GOLF
THE CURE FOR A GRUMPY OLD MAN

Illustrated by Chris Perfect

Best Wishes Dennis.

GOLF

THE CURE FOR A GRUMPY OLD MAN

PETER ALLISS

HODDER

First published in Great Britain in 2008 by Hodder & Stoughton
An Hachette UK company

First published in paperback in 2009

7

A CIP catalogue record for this title is available from the British Library

ISBN 978 0 340 97863 4

Typeset in Galliard by Eric Drewery

Printed and bound by Clays Ltd, St Ives plc

Hodder & Stoughton policy is to use papers that are natural, renewable
and recyclable products and made from wood grown in sustainable
forests. The logging and manufacturing processes are expected to
conform to the environmental regulations of the country of origin.

Hodder & Stoughton Ltd
338 Euston Road
London NW1 3BH

www.hodder.co.uk

To the glorious game of golf

CONTENTS

CONTENTS

ACKNOWLEDGEMENTS

I would like to express my warm thanks to Chris Perfect, who provided the excellent instructional drawings, to Dominicq Hoy, my long-suffering PA, to physiotherapists Elizabeth Sharp and Darren Norman for their invaluable tips to the older golfer on getting and staying fit, to Andy Farrell for ably editing my manuscript and to my publisher Roddy Bloomfield, with whom I have now worked on five books without any undue grumpiness on either side. My thanks to Betty Dobereiner and Sarah Wooldridge for welcoming the inclusion of extracts by their much-loved husbands Peter Dobereiner and Ian Wooldridge. They were wonderful sports journalists for the *Observer* and the *Daily Mail*.

PICTURE
ACKNOWLEDGEMENTS

The author and publisher would like to thank the following for permission to reproduce photographs:

Robert Beck/Getty Images, Robyn Beck/Getty Images, David Cannon/Getty Images, Stuart Franklin/Getty Images, Hobbs Golf Collection, Travis Lindquist/Getty Images, Warren Little/Getty Images, Bob Martin/Getty Images, Tom Mihalek/Getty Images, Phil Sheldon Golf Picture Library.

Every reasonable effort has been made to contact the copyright holders, but if there are any errors or omissions, Hodder & Stoughton will be pleased to insert the appropriate acknowledgement in any subsequent printing of this publication.

FOREWORD

Ian Wooldridge

When 16-year-old Henry Alliss brought some school friends home the other day, he introduced them to his father thus: 'This is Dad. He shouts a bit, but he's okay really.'

Shouts a bit? Could this be the hidden alter ego of the honey-tongued BBC golf commentator whose brief flash of irascibility during this year's Open Championship deluged *Sportsmail* with the biggest response to any poll it has ever conducted?

More than 2,000 readers wrote in. And by a seven-to-one consensus the verdict was: 'Lay off Alliss. He represents standards of behaviour our country is fast losing.'

The dissenters called him pompous or reactionary, sometimes both.

Alliss replied to his accusers with a smile. 'I quite understand that,' he said. 'Anyone over fifty in Britain today is regarded as a dinosaur. If you still stand up when a woman walks into the room, they think you're completely daft.'

It was the hottest day of the year when we met at Wentworth. He was wearing a jacket and tie and was ten minutes early for our interview. He is so punctilious about such matters and much else that it seemed appropriate to invite him to list the things he dislikes most in the sixty-ninth year of his very public life.

He was up and running in a flash: 'Graffiti, vandalism, bad manners, road rage, riding bicycles on pavements, very bad language on television, rude and uncontrolled children, parents who let their children run riot, inconsiderate people who slam hotel doors at unsocial hours, poor teachers, schools with no discipline, all-night television, excessive nationalism and almost everything now regarded as politically correct.'

So what *does* he like?

'British humour, solid stone houses, orderly queueing, good manners, fish and chips, fair play, dogs, discipline, honesty, Scotch whisky, kindly eccentricity, pine trees, rhododendrons, bikinis, Bournemouth, Cadbury's chocolate and coal or wood fires in wintertime.'

Young Henry Alliss, the youngest of Peter's six children from two marriages – one, Victoria, died tragically at the age of twelve – clearly has a rigorous agenda to live up to.

'Well, I suppose I've shouted at all of them from time to time,' says his father, 'and if you ask them whether I was a disciplinarian they'd probably say I was dramatically so.

'But so what? They don't go around abusing things or people. They all come home as often as possible. The house is always full of laughter. Is that so bad? And isn't it nice when someone comes up to you and says: "I met a couple of your kids the other day. They were charming."'

The house is approached by a longish drive in six acres of land in Hindhead, Surrey, and has six bedrooms and two full-time gardeners. It is closer to London's airports than his beloved Bournemouth, and Alliss still commutes almost three months each year to commentate in America, as well as following golf all over Europe.

His idea of relaxing when at home is to have a few friends

in for dinner. The hospitality is legendary. You don't drink the latest supermarket bargain.

The chatelaine on these occasions is his wife, Jackie. She is small, dynamic and hugely protective of her husband's reputation. She is also a JP on the Surrey bench at Guildford, a governor of a local school, runs a charity to raise funds for the detection of tumours and, for relaxation, pilots her shared small private plane. She is currently on holiday with some of the Alliss children at their other place in southern Spain.

None of these manifestations of middle-class comfort was attained from a silver-spoon upbringing. Peter Alliss, son of a fine professional tournament golfer, Percy, left grammar school at fourteen. Well, at fourteen and three-quarters actually, but still too young to contemplate university or the conventional professions.

'There was another contributory factor to the way I think now,' said Alliss. 'I was brought up in the Second World War years when nothing could be taken for granted, not even your life, and nothing could be wasted.

'You didn't leave lights on all over the house. You had one bar of chocolate a month. And even after the war, when you took a girl out, you had to get the last bus home at 10.30 or trudge ten miles. These days, driving lessons at sixteen, a gift car at seventeen and a gap year touring around the Far East before going to university seem to be regarded as a birthright. I simply don't understand it.'

At fifteen, Alliss played in the prestigious British Boys' Golf Championship, became an assistant to his father at the Ferndown Golf Club in Dorset, left for two years' National Service and returned to become a professional tournament golfer. He played in eight Ryder Cups, ten World Cups and every Open Championship until 1974.

Becoming a television commentator never crossed his mind.

'Extraordinary how these things happen,' he said. 'In 1970

I'd played pretty well in a tournament in Dublin and on the plane coming home I was probably on a high and regaling my neighbours with stories about the hilarious things that can happen to you in Ireland.

'A few weeks later I was approached by Ray Lakeland, a northern BBC chap who produced sports programmes on rugby union, rugby league, cricket and golf. Ray said: "I was sitting just behind you on the plane back from Dublin the other day. I heard everything you said. Why not come and have a go at television?"'

Alliss did. At first, he provided short comments for insertion into long transmissions; then, after his final Open Championship appearance in 1974, he was invited to join the full commentary team headed by the magisterial Henry Longhurst, a short, squat man who hated appearing on camera. For the next fourteen years Alliss fronted TV's *Pro-Celebrity Golf*. For the second time in his life he was a national figure.

Never has he fallen into the celebrity trap that destroys so many febrile TV front-persons before they've learned some three syllable words from the dictionary.

'By choice,' said Alliss, 'I would prefer to arrive at and depart from golf tournaments by submarine.'

He comes up with ad-lib phrases like that all through his golf commentaries. 'I have no idea where they come from,' he said. 'They just happen.'

He is as uncompromising about golf as he was about the upbringing of his children. On TV, he briefly criticized Frenchman Jean Van de Velde, who made such a hash of the last hole of the Open Championship at Carnoustie, and makes no apology for it: 'I have seen amateur players at St Andrews and Gleneagles go out there and take air-shots off the first tee. What in God's name are they doing there?'

Alliss, unashamedly, does not like the second rate.

His youngest son, Henry, is named to honour three of Peter's greatest friends: the late Sir Henry Cotton, supreme golfer; the late Henry Longhurst, emeritus of the English language; and Henry Cooper, the Cockney rough diamond who became the first man to horizontalize Muhammad Ali, and who has, with his lovely wife Albina, richly contributed to British public life.

'You know what all these three very different men had in common?' queried Alliss. 'In their own very different ways, they had style. They epitomised our country at its very best.'

Thus an insight into the mind of Peter Alliss, a man who deplores what is happening to our country. His greatest credential is that he is no commercial fat cat. He has earned his every penny the hard way.

Sarah Wooldridge comments: 'My husband, Ian, was a long-standing friend of Peter Alliss; he would have been delighted to see his article, first published in the *Daily Mail* in 1999, reproduced as the foreword to this book.'

August 2008

1

GOLF AND THE
GRUMPY OLD MAN

*'It is this constant and undying hope for improvement that
makes golf so exquisitely worth the playing.'*
BERNARD DARWIN, golf writer

So you recognise yourself as a Grumpy Old Man. Or, at least,
you have been told you are becoming a Grumpy Old Man,
even if only by being given this book! In either case you are
reluctantly accepting that you are a man of a certain age,
beginning to feel disappointed that life is rushing by, and that
you are having to run harder to stand still. Your mobility is on
the wane and, with your knee problems, tennis, squash and
cricket are out of the question.

Don't worry, there is a cure for your malaise and it's right
here in front of you. No, my friend, it's not snake oil
(although that's pretty useful for the old joints), it's not
euthanasia (too drastic) ... it's golf.

Now you may already be a golfer with a spiralling handicap,

or you may not yet have played the game, but, either way, I shall reveal to you how to wave this magic wand and bring back the sparkle to your life.

Before you take the cure, I just need to ask you a few personal questions and give you a quick examination. Have you recently noticed:

a lack of energy
a decrease in your strength and endurance
that you are becoming sad or grumpy
a deterioration in your sports ability
a decrease in your sex drive
that you fall asleep in the day

No, you don't have to feel embarrassed. Of course the answer is yes to all of them; we diagnosticians call it the andropause. And you probably also think you can't trust politicians, that the roads are overcrowded, that kids have no manners, that dustbins aren't emptied often enough and that petrol tax is too high. In all of which cases you are of course perfectly right, although here I think I am unlikely to help. What I can prescribe for you however will undoubtedly assist you in coping with some of those personal problems you confessed to a moment ago:

- Find new ways to relieve stress – join a golf club or renew your existing membership or find a pay-and-play golf club, or just start off at the local driving range
- Eat a low-fat high-fibre diet – avoid the golf club steward's 'Today's Special'
- Exercise regularly – three rounds of golf a week should do the trick
- Talk about your problems with friends – not during the round but later at the bar
- Limit your consumption of alcohol and caffeine before you go out for a round of golf
- Drink lots of water – with your whisky at the golf club.

That should give you a good start. Now all you need to do is to keep it up and read the following chapters and you just may be completely cured. Now everything that follows applies equally to women as to men, so hopefully, this book will help anyone who is thinking of taking up this wonderful game, or who needs to regain the sparkle in their golf.

2

WHY GOLF IS THE CURE

'Golf is the only sport where a man [of] sixty can play with the best. That's why golf is such a great game.'
SAM SNEAD, *Golf Digest*, 1975

How can golf be the cure for the Grumpy Old Man? Surely, this is a combustible combination: one of the most frustrating games ever invented and people who are only too aware of the frustrations that life throws up. You only have to look at some of those who play the game for a living. Take Colin Montgomerie. Dear old Monty, he can be the most charming dinner companion and a genial host – his recent wedding at Loch Lomond went off wonderfully – but if there is a crisp packet rustling somewhere in the same county, the perpetrator can expect the most withering glare imaginable. Or if you have to talk to him after he has bogeyed the 18th hole, forget it. Certainly getting in his way is like throwing yourself under a steamroller. Of course, Monty will have stopped emitting steam only a few moments later but by then it has been known for him to be halfway down the motorway still in his golf spikes.

Monty, however, is a pussy cat compared to the old firebrand Tommy Bolt, who was well known for throwing clubs and even breaking them over his knee. But a couple of times Tommy got his comeuppance. Once he was arguing with a caddie about which club to use for his approach to a green. Bolt thought it was a five-iron, the caddie insisted it was a six. Tommy took out the five-iron and hit his ball twenty yards over the green. Furious, he snapped the five-iron over his knee. The caddie meanwhile, not too happy himself, promptly snapped the six-iron over his own knee, dropped Bolt's bag and walked off the course.

Another time, Bolt was playing well in the opening round of the US Open at Cherry Hills in 1960. But on the back nine his game fell apart. He drove out of bounds on one hole, then into a pond on the next. His mood was not helped by him losing a heated dispute with a rules official over where to drop his ball, and by the time he reached the 18th green, after a string of bogeys, Bolt was fuming. The tee shot required a carry over a lake and, inevitably, it did not make it to dry ground. Neither did the second ball, which was all too much for Tommy. Winding up with a swing fuelled by pure rage, Bolt hurled his driver into the water too. With quick thinking, a small boy in the gallery dived into the lake and amazingly retrieved the driver. He emerged from the water with the club over his head and even Bolt finally had to break into a smile as he went to thank the boy for finding his favourite club. But immediately the boy broke into a run, skipped past Bolt, sped across the fairway and, after getting help over the chain link fence enclosing the property from another spectator, disappeared for ever.

> *'A cardinal rule for the club breaker is never break your putter and driver in the same match or you are dead.'*
> TOMMY BOLT,
> *How to Keep Your Temper on the Golf Course*, 1969

Tommy Bolt may have been a one-off but golf has its fair share of strange characters. Even Nick Faldo, unquestionably the finest British golfer of the last sixty years, appeared so obsessed with the game that he could come across as aloof and uncommunicative – in complete contrast to the persona who now inhabits the commentary box at tournaments in America. As for Tiger Woods, the world's best golfer has lost count of the number of times he has been in trouble for swearing on national television. Let's face it, there is so much that can go wrong on a golf course that there is the potential for the game to be an endless source of irritation. All that guff about taking the rough with the smooth, who needs it?

Well, Tiger, for one, shows us exactly how to react. He can be furious for a moment but then immediately switches to thinking about what he is going to do with the next shot. How he got there doesn't matter any more. All that matters is the shot about to be played. And that's the point about golf, you can't replay the last shot, but you can do something about the next one – a bit like life, wouldn't you say?

But here is the real secret of golf – good players may go away remembering the odd poor shot, but poor players only remember the good ones. And that's enough to get the grumpiest of grumps smiling with contentment.

But don't take my word for it.

Quite independently from the idea for this book, researches in Sweden have discovered that playing golf can add five years to your life! Professor Anders Ahlbom, from the Karolinska Institute in Stockholm, revealed, after studying 500,000 golfers, that the game has greater health benefits than walking and even more strenuous forms of exercise. He told the *Daily Telegraph*: 'A round of golf means being outside for about four hours, walking at a fast pace for six to seven kilometres, something which is good for the health. People play golf into old age, and there are also positive social and psychological aspects to the game that can be of help.'

Apparently, and this might interest you, the lowest death rates were recorded for low-handicap golfers, who are 47 per cent less likely to die at any time than non-golfers of the same age. Our Swedish scientist added: 'Maintaining a low handicap involves playing a lot, so this supports the idea that it is the game itself that is good for the health.'

If that is not an incentive to not only take up the game but try and get as good as you can, I don't know what is. So, what about it? I confess I can't wave a magic wand without you putting in some effort. But if I can introduce a new way of thinking to those who have played a long time and are losing their power, and a way for beginners of a certain maturity to go forward with a view to enjoying the game for many years, then it will all be worthwhile.

All it takes is one shot. It might be a drive that disappears into the stratosphere, an approach shot that nestles next to the hole, a recovery shot from a bunker that explodes from the sand over the high lip and back to safety on the green or a putt holed to win a match. Nothing feels better and that is the secret that even the grumpiest of golfers understands. It is the shot that brings you back the next time and the next. If the object of the exercise is to move the ball from point A to point B, then there are times when not even the combined talents of Tiger Woods, Seve Ballesteros, Nick Faldo and Jack Nicklaus could have done it more effectively – with more style or finesse, sure, but, remember, unlike in ice skating, there are no points for technical merit or artistic impression. It's not how but how many.

Wherever I go on my travels in the world I am asked what the appeal of the game is, and I sometimes warn those asking the questions that it can often be annoying, frustrating and even infuriating. But anyone who has actually played the game knows that the joy of hitting one great shot – one that feels just right, or does exactly what was intended, or is helped by an outrageous bounce or good fortune – far outweighs all the bad ones. Despite the drawbacks, golf is a game to be enjoyed.

There are many reasons for this: the surroundings, often beautiful, always better than being stuck indoors; the handicapping system that allows players of differing standards to compete against each other; different formats that offer a variety of competitions; and the general sociability of being a member of a club and, in particular, at the 19th hole. It is a game for all ages, in all weathers, on all terrains. Perhaps there can be no greater endorsement than the literally hundreds upon hundreds of men and women who, like many of you reading this book may go on to do, have taken up the game relatively late in life. Whether they achieve a little or a great deal of success, with one voice they come to me and say, 'Oh, how I wish I'd started earlier!'

Usually, they have been active in other sports and have only come to golf when their abilities at more strenuous sports began to wane. Then there are others who have played no sport at all since leaving school. The waist has expanded a little and the spouse or doctor has said, 'You must really take some exercise.' I make no bones about it. Golf is very good exercise indeed. It fulfils key government health objectives of getting people on their feet and out in the fresh air. The average golf course is over 6,000 yards long, further when you include walks between green and tee, with more to be added when, alas, the ball flies none too straight. You will also be carrying a bag of clubs or pulling a trolley over usually undulating ground. Finally, there is the game itself, which involves swinging a club in a way that brings into use about every muscle in the body.

If you are starting later in life, I am not about to argue that you have a chance of matching the achievements of a Bobby Jones or a Jack Nicklaus. Or a Tiger Woods, for that matter. Tiger's first experience of golf was watching from his high chair as his late father, Earl, swung a club in front of him. Soon, by which I mean by the age of nine months, the wee cub was having a go at swinging a club himself. By comparison, it seems that I was a late beginner, first swinging a club at the age of twenty months, and I have never stopped learning about the game since. So, although I don't want to try to persuade you that you can begin late and still be great, I would argue that a late beginner can become highly competent and have year after year of enjoyment. After all, there are examples of people still playing at a ripe old age, certainly into their nineties and no doubt still canny putters.

Eventually, of course, extreme age will set a limit, but for many retired from work a round of golf perhaps a couple of times a week remains an enduring pleasure. There are many indeed who have not taken up the game until this stage in their lives. Before that there were the pressures of work, a family to bring up, the garden to tend. Not until retirement has there been time in plenty to spare. Even this is not too late, particularly, perhaps, for those who have had good ball sense in their youth. If you start in your sixties, you are unlikely to become a club champion, but with a handicap perhaps in the high teens and an enthusiasm for the game you will still be able to do what golf is all about: enjoy yourself.

And what better place to enjoy yourself than on a golf course. Any game has drawbacks and can be thought of as a stupid waste of time but there is no denying that, as my late colleague and friend Henry Longhurst used to say, 'Golf takes you to such beautiful places.'

Many courses are laid out on land by no means designed by nature for the game. At worst, I have sometimes found nothing more than a flat, cold, clay field with views of factory chimneys, cramped Victorian housing or even a prison wall. Yet there will still be a few birds aloft, trees growing and the feeling of being in the open air. Indeed, by far the majority of courses in the British Isles and elsewhere are set in far more attractive landscapes. Many are a delight to all the senses.

You may have come across Dylan Thomas's poem 'Fern Hill', in which he recalls his youthful visits to a Welsh farm. I grew up from the age of seven at a golf club with a similar name, Ferndown, some six miles north of Bournemouth on the Dorset–Hampshire border. My father, Percy Alliss, a travelling Yorkshireman who had jobs in Wales, Buckinghamshire, Yorkshire, Essex and even Berlin, where I was born, came there in 1938 and remained as a professional until the late 1960s. It was there and on other courses in the Bournemouth area that my golf game developed. My liking for birch and pine woodland has never left me. I was not a keen ornithologist, nor did I know the proper botanical names for the many wild flowers, but the feeling of the still glades – even after taking three putts – has always remained with me.

As my game progressed, I began to play on courses further afield. Today, if faced with the choice, I would play out my days in the golfing landscape of my roots, a few miles from our Ferndown home those many years ago.

Many golfers would disagree with me. For them, the great delight of golf is those rather barren stretches of land hard by the sea, with rearing sand dunes, rushes, gulls shrieking and whirling and the crash of waves on the shore. For many, links golf is the only real golf, and they scorn courses that meander amongst ancient oaks or carve their way through pine forest. The British Isles is fortunate in its wealth of links terrain. It is found along the Kent and Lancashire coasts, in eastern and western Scotland and elsewhere. If kept in good condition, the turf seems designed by nature for a golf ball to lie neat and clean, asking to be struck. The bunkering may be entirely natural or only need the surface to be scraped away. The greens ought to be fast and true – even in winter – but subtly undulating. Nowhere else will the golfer be so closely in touch with the weather. Inland, the day may be still and humid, but on links land there is always the freshness of the seas and a light breeze. For some lovers of links golf, working the ball low into a stiff north-easterly is the thing. Others relish a soft summer evening with the skylarks swooping overhead.

But, of course, golf has long since spread inland. I am not prepared to enter into the argument over whether our game owes its birth to the medieval *kolven* of Holland or originated in Scotland. However, there's no doubt that it was the Scots who spread the game throughout Britain and around the world. Golf has come to be played in every type of landscape. There are courses on Japanese mountainsides, in Burmese jungles, in the desert, manufactured by huge earth-moving machines in America, in rolling parkland, on downs where the wind blows free, and on the heaths of Surrey, Yorkshire and Germany. Only the communist states resisted the appeal of golf but of course that has now changed, not only in eastern Europe and Russia but in China, where the game is suddenly booming. Who could have thought that there would be more tournaments on the European Tour in China than in Scotland. It's a weird and wonderful world!

If you are looking to join a golf club, many factors will come into play, such as how far away it is – if popping down and playing just a few holes on a summer's evening or hitting a few chips and putts around the practice green appeals, then the closer the better – whether you know people who are already members, or what the clubhouse facilities are like. But however far away it is, it is worth bearing in mind that golf in surroundings that give you a lift, however badly you may be playing on a particular day, is to be preferred. On the other hand, there are more and more golfers these days who opt not to join just one club but pay-and-play at different venues. Ask the pro at your nearby club or driving range what the options are for this sort of membership locally. This variety will help to develop your game and may also better suit those who still have a busy schedule or a limited budget.

One question you may be asking yourself, if you have never played the game before, is how difficult is golf? There is no hard and fast answer. Undoubtedly it is one of the most difficult games to play to a very high standard. Every course is different, and even when playing the same course all the time – as many golfers do – you will find that it is wholly or subtly different from one day to another, or even from hour to hour. You may find yourself in winter or summer trying to keep your hands and club grips dry, while pulling a trolley, holding an umbrella, and writing down the score to boot. In golf, play is abandoned only if the course becomes unplayable through flooding or snow cover or presents a danger to life from lightning. No concession is made to the players' comfort!

People coming to golf from sports which involve reflex actions and a moving ball find it difficult. It looks so much easier. There is that little white ball quietly waiting to be hit. It's all up to you. Nothing your opponent can do should affect your own ability to swing the club back and through. I remember Prince Philip saying to me that he hadn't taken up golf because it was, 'Too easy. Try polo. That's hitting a ball with a club, but it's moving and you've got to ride a horse as well.' True enough, but in the little polo I have watched, I noticed that they missed the ball a lot and the pony seemed to do all the work.

In many sports you have no time to think of the consequences of what you are about to do. A ball hurtles towards you and you react instinctively. But what happens when the player has got time to think? There's the penalty in soccer, for instance. Whoever takes a penalty has quite a long time to think how easy it ought to be to place the ball in the net, but many penalty kicks go rather feebly straight to the goalkeeper. The kicker has not kept his nerve. The horrid thoughts of failure have got to him. In rugby, similarly, most things happen at a fairly high speed – but you need nerve at fullback as a high up-and-under is hoisted into the air. How frightful to drop it in front of a packed house at Twickenham with a historic win against the All Blacks in the balance! Or think of tennis. The players dart about the court and the ball flashes to and fro across the net, sometimes in a marvellous volleying sequence too fast for the eye to follow. But what happens when a player is serving? Now he is almost in a golf situation: he or she has to toss the ball gently in the air and strike it when almost stationary. How often are double faults served in a crisis of the match? And finally cricket on the village green. The fast bowlers have had their say and the score is clicking along nicely. The fielding team is glum. Oh well, let's give old Charlie a go. Old Charlie ambles up to the wicket and sends down his standard delivery: a lob up in the air that takes some time to reach the batsman. 'Easy,' thinks he. That is just the trouble. He does have time to think – and time to doubt and change his mind. Another wicket for old Charlie.

So, then, golf is a very difficult game to play to a high standard, but it is one of the easiest games to play well enough to enjoy. After all, the ball is stationary. You don't need much natural reflex ability or great strength to see you through. Strength can be a disadvantage. My father once taught an Olympic weightlifter who never succeeded in hitting a golf ball more than 180 yards despite his strength. Never was a man more frustrated and eventually he gave up the game.

The ability you most need to hit a golf ball long and far is that of making a clubhead move fast, to accelerate it. Other considerations come into striking a golf ball a long way, but you must get the clubhead moving fast. But don't despair, it doesn't take great strength or clubhead speed to move the ball over 200 yards and that will be enough for you to be able to compete enjoyably at golf. Hand and arm speed are undoubtedly very important and later I shall be explaining a few ways in which these can be improved, although they depend to some extent on how naturally gifted you are. But you must be prepared to give the necessary time to developing your game.

If you have been successful at other ball games you will begin with certain advantages. Above all, you will have learned how to *compete*, how to keep your nerve in a crisis in a match, how to steel yourself to play a shot when you lack confidence in your ability to play it. You will also have to unlearn some of the skills you bring to golf from other sports. All manner of marvellous shots, for instance, can be played at racquet games when the player is off-balance, but in golf an off-balance shot is seldom a good one. The basic mechanics of the swing must always be right. Nevertheless, such people have already one of the essentials of golf: how to swing an implement *through* the ball not merely *at* it.

I would always, for instance, back a good-class cricket batsman to attain a relatively low golf handicap. Certainly driving a ball straight for six, with a full backswing and follow-through, closely resembles what we are after in the golf swing. Even so, the cricket backswing is much shorter than that necessary for golf – indeed, some players have no backswing at all. Many golfers, such as Bernard Hunt and Doug Sanders, prospered with short backswings – barely to the vertical – but such short swings often cause problems, particularly as regards rhythm, an essential ingredient in golf.

My father, Percy, had an encouraging message for beginners. Unlike me, he reckoned it was an easy game. It was 'us' who made it difficult, particularly through not accepting limitations and allowing little or no time at all for practice.

The most famous hole in golf? The 19th, of course, yet it has little if anything to do with the game. It's the favoured place in the clubhouse for a drink and companionship. After the game is over, the conversation flows over an orange juice or whatever you fancy. For many, this part of the golfing day – especially if the golf has not prospered – may prove to be the most enjoyable. Here every man and woman becomes an expert – in their eyes at least! We can complain that the new sand being tried out in the bunkers is really quite unsuitable – 'Why don't they use the same kind as at so-and-so golf club?' 'Why, for heaven's sake, haven't they started to scarify the greens yet, and why is that green-keeper planting all those trees just where my drive normally finishes at the 14th?' 'This new handicapping system is dreadful. The wrong people seem to be winning all the competitions.' 'What do you think of this new steward they've got hold of? Do you know, he refused to get me bacon and eggs at 4 a.m. when the card school broke up.' 'The new secretary's a tartar. Ordered me out of the bar last week because I still had my golf shoes on. Fellow seemed to think I was dropping grass and mud all over the place. It's just like being at home.' 'Who's that lady member? Haven't seen her before. Is she new? Mmm, might ask her to play in the mixed foursomes next week.'

The talk ranges freely. Few topics are actually banned, though perhaps politics should be treated with caution. There's one subject above all to be avoided. No one, absolutely no one, is interested in how you played your last round. You have to be Woods or Els in a crowded press tent to find an interested audience, and even they have long ago learned that their fellow players care not in the least. As the great Bobby Locke used to say in kindly tones, 'How did you play today, Master – but please start at the 18th!'

I learned this lesson myself many years ago. I was in the company of my father, the Whitcombe brothers and Abe Mitchell, the greatest player to fail to win the Open Championship. Into the clubhouse came a dejected young man, Bill Laidlaw, an assistant to Henry Cotton at Ashridge. He was a most promising player whose career never came to fruition only because he was killed in the war. Seeing his dejection, Abe Mitchell said, 'What's the matter, son?' This was a mistake. Bill proceeded to go through his round stroke by horrid stroke. There was the opening drive out of bounds, an iron shot ruled on the flag that kicked sharp right into a pot bunker, a four-putt where the hole had been set just at the top of a rise and the ball returned to Bill's feet rather too often. So the account went on, the minutes ticked away. But we heard him out. When the tale of disaster came to an end, the generally kind Abe Mitchell leaned forward and said, 'Yes, it's a sad story, lad. But remember this, no one but you gives a bugger.'

So, dear friends, take heed. It's a self-centred world. Don't launch into a wordy account of the state of the game, and if anyone asks you how went the day, limit your reply to a dozen words. Perhaps, 'Not bad, but I couldn't get a putt,' or 'Had four birdies,' or 'Couldn't have hit my hat,' or 'Thirty-three on the outward half and 52 home.' That will be quite enough for your audience, unless you are a raconteur accustomed to having your fellow men rolling in the aisles. Otherwise, let the conversation flow where it will. And flow it will. What a game it is for meeting new friends and the most interesting people.

3

1608 AND ALL THAT

'I never could hit that fairway.'
Walker Cup golfer 'Laddie' Lucas after crash-landing his
Spitfire during air strikes over the Channel in 1941 beside
the ninth fairway at Prince's Club in Kent, where his
father was the secretary.

If golf is to be your new hobby it's not a bad thing to know a little bit of its history, although even some people who earn their living from the game do not seem to appreciate this. Some time ago I was hosting the Men v Women golf series from Woburn Golf and Country Club. We were staying in some style at the Bell Hotel in the little town of Aston Clinton. On this particular occasion two of the players involved were Greg Norman, the Australian, and the top woman golfer in the world at that time, Nancy Lopez.

One night after dinner, when it was coffee time and the cigars were being passed round, Nancy Lopez suddenly asked me the name of my favourite golfer, or one who in my opinion was 'king of the castle'. I ran off a few, starting with Bobby Jones and his great feats in the 1920s and early '30s, Walter Hagen, Ben Hogan, of course the impact that Arnold Palmer, Gary Player and Jack Nicklaus had on the game, then I said I had a great respect for the South African, Bobby Locke, and added I wished he was around today to see how he would get on with such power golfers as Greg Norman, Tom Watson, Ray Floyd and the like. In my opinion, I thought, pound for pound, he was possibly one of the greatest players the world of golf had ever seen.

Her face went blank and she uttered the immortal words, 'Who is Bobby Locke?'

It was a very sobering moment. I often wonder how many players today take the trouble of looking back to see who did what and where. I get the feeling if Tiger Woods ever found himself in a quiz concerning all things golf he'd know most of the answers, he's that sort of fellow, a rare talent, a remarkable mind. All that and blessed, most of the time, with good luck. An unbeatable combination.

So, you'll be wanting to know something of the game's history and the extraordinary things which have happened since records were kept. So much has been written about golf, a game so different from any other, its characters, its humour, the situations, the majestic surroundings players enjoy. Here is a brief history of the game and a few facts and figures, which I hope will entertain, amuse and educate you.

The beginnings of the game are shrouded in mystery. We are told Mary Queen of Scots was out knocking a ball about on the banks of the Firth of Forth whilst her dear husband was being decapitated. Strange woman! How callous!

So you see, there are records going back 500 years. I'm absolutely certain that one day someone will discover an ancient tomb in the Middle East and there, carved on the walls, will be stick-like figures, waving something that could be a club and trying to hit a spherical object that might be a ball. That might be several thousand years before Christ. Were that ever to happen it would upset the pundits who categorically state they can put their finger on where this mystical game began!

The game was moving along, albeit fairly slowly, in the eighteenth century and there are many pictures of landowners of the day standing proudly, hand on hip, grasping some strange-looking implement, waiting to step out and challenge the meagre golf links of the day.

Although the Scots fiercely claim to be the inventors of the game, there are some very old paintings depicting a game similar to golf played on the frozen lakes of Holland. There's no doubt a stick-and-ball game was played there many moons ago but whether or not it was quite like the game of golf is not certain.

In the eighteenth century the first set of rules was drawn up by members of the Honourable Company of Edinburgh Golfers, better known as Muirfield, situated on the banks of the Firth of Forth some twenty-five miles east of the fair city of Edinburgh. Little did they think when they put those few words on paper that the game would explode the way it has, now creating a book of rules that rivals the size of the Bible. The first Open Championship was played in 1860 on the west coast of Scotland at Prestwick. They only had 12 holes in those days, the first one was over 600 yards and Old Tom Morris opened up with a three! Three full-blooded shots and it disappeared down the hole. Quite amazing, because the course must have been very unsophisticated, and goodness knows how big the hole was. Remember, this was long before the invention of the steel sleeve which nowadays is sunk into the ground, leaving a gap of a couple of inches or so round the top to cushion the ball before it, hopefully, disappears from view.

There were eight entries, in fact that was the number who played the first three years the championship was in operation, then it leapt up to fourteen and, apart from a few hiccups, the number of players increased until 1901, when, for the first time, more than a hundred players participated. By 1939, on the verge of World War Two breaking out, that number had risen to 254. Now in the twenty-first century there are a number of qualifying venues throughout the world and the actual total of entries runs into thousands.

The Royal Blackheath Club was founded in 1608. It was round about this time the Scottish king succeeded to the throne of England (James VI of Scotland became James I of England). Back in those early days records weren't always kept, so although tradition has it that Blackheath started in 1608, the really solid evidence doesn't come in until 1787. The earliest evidence of golf at the Royal Burgess Golfing Society of Edinburgh was April 1773; also the earliest written evidence of golf at the Royal and Ancient (R&A) at Edinburgh is 14 May 1754. Scotland still continued to dominate the world of golf in those early days; it wasn't until 1818 that there was evidence of another golf course in England and that was Old Manchester.

I'm sure many of you wonder how and why the preface 'Royal' is featured in the name of a number of golf clubs. Currently there are over sixty clubs worldwide entitled to use the word 'Royal' in their address. The first club to get royal patronage was the Perth Golfing Society in 1833; next came the Royal and Ancient Golf Club of St Andrews in 1834; then almost seventy years passed before Aberdeen had a royal patron in the person of the future Edward VII. Most recent was the Royal Mayfair Club in Edmonton, Canada, which received its royal status in 2005. What do you have to do to get the royal title? Usually, a member of the royal household comes and has a game and the club secretary or powers that be write to say they were so delighted to entertain Your Highness or Your Majesty, and please could they now go on to be listed as a royal club? In other words, a member of the royal family has to have played on their course.

The most prolific royal golfer and donor of royal titles was George V who bestowed the title to the Royal Burgess Golfing Society on the outskirts of Edinburgh in 1929. Over the centuries quite a number of royals have been interested in the game of golf – the Dukes of York and Kent played in the 1930s, the Duke of York becoming King George VI after the abdication of his brother, the Duke of Windsor in the mid-1930s. Now there was a man who loved his golf in his wilderness years after his abdication.

It is interesting to note that Scotland, which, for want of discussion, fostered the game of golf, does have a number of very élitist clubs. But golf has always been a game for the people and this was brought home to me as long ago as 1946 when I went to Edinburgh to play in the Boys Championship, aged fifteen. My father was my chaperon and we went very slowly from Bournemouth to Edinburgh on the train, then caught the bus out to Bruntsfield, which was two or three miles west of the city. There were actually people getting on to the bus carrying golf clubs. Nobody looked at them as if they were a bit weird, though the looks would be very different if you attempted to carry golf clubs on the Underground in London.

Golf now is huge business, and there are thousands of courses around the world, some of them in the strangest places. There are a number of golf courses in Britain situated well over 1,000 feet above sea level, a number in Wales and Herefordshire, among them Llandrindod Wells at over 1,000 feet, Church Stretton at 1,250 feet, and Tredegar at 1,300 feet. As you would expect, the highest golf courses in Europe are in the Alps – Crans-sur-Sierre, where they play the Swiss

Open Championship (now the European Masters), and Sestrières in the Italian Alps, both at well over 6,000 feet. Around the globe, the highest regular golf courses are to be found in Bolivia. There, there's a course 11,000 feet above sea level, and in La Paz, the capital, there's one which looks down upon the world from a height of 12,000 feet. Pioneers of yesteryear have played golf in the upper reaches of Tibet, a certain Captain E. S. Adair, a golfing enthusiast who always travelled with a couple of clubs in his luggage, made a one-hole course to liven up his lonely hours, probably the first time this wonderful ancient game was played at an elevation in excess of 16,000 feet.

If that's the highest, whereabouts would we find the lowest? Well, it was at a place called Kalia, south of Jericho. Believe it or not, it was 1,250 feet below normal sea level. The course ran all round the northern shore of the Dead Sea and was created by the Kalia Hotel. It was built on sand and shingle so the clubs took a bit of a bashing, and the Dead Sea is one of the hottest areas in the world. But it was pleasant during the winter months and well suited to golf; you could always stop and have a bathe in its dense waters. Even if your game was so bad that you jumped in, it would be impossible to drown, so there's some compensation!

Would you believe it, a Scotsman founded the Polar Bear Club in the Arctic, where Eskimos became members. As the world's most northerly golf club, it was always below zero due to the eternal snow and ice, and once the course was closed for a three-year period! An Arbroath golfer named Munro Sievwright did not neglect his practice meanwhile. With two or three clubs and a dozen or so golf balls, which he painted red, in the light of the midnight sun he hit a number of shots into the white wastelands of the fairways, which, after all, were just hard-packed snow. Years ago there was a course in northern Kenya 10,000 feet above sea level, and a number of golf courses in India and Sri Lanka were created in excess of 6,500 feet above sea level. Perhaps the majestic course at Banff Springs, Alberta, Canada, is the most glamorous of all, an 18-hole course at 4,500 feet above sea level. It is surrounded on all sides by towering snow-capped mountains and mighty trees – absolutely magnificent.

In America, California, because of its moderate climate, was blessed with a number of golf courses; but over the last fifty or sixty years the deserts of New Mexico and Arizona, not to mention Palm Springs, a hundred miles east of Los Angeles, have become huge playgrounds of the rich and famous, and perhaps those not so rich, through the advent of golf courses. I remember that when I first visited Palm Springs in the early 1950s, there were only three or four golf courses, but now the number is approaching 150. In fact, there are so many they are actually changing the climate. How? Well, with the advent of more golf courses and sophisticated green-keeping methods, courses were fully irrigated; more people came to live in the area causing thousands of swimming pools to be created. The heat sucked the water into the atmosphere and, lo and behold, over a fairly short period condensation and humidity were created where, a hundred years ago, there was none.

The blame can be placed very firmly at the door of the travelling Scots and the diplomatic corps. A large number of Scots occupied places in the world of politics and engineering, spreading their skills across the world and managing to take their golf clubs and balls with them to set up courses wherever they laid their heads – South America, Africa, India, Japan and most stations north, east, south and west. Those of us who love the game should go on bended knee and thank them for their love of the game, which turned out to be wonderful foresight.

The Royal and Ancient, based at St Andrews, is the ruling body in the world of golf outside the USA and Mexico, and operates in 120 countries on behalf of an estimated 130 million golfers in Europe, Africa and Asia, and South America. In 1952 the R&A and the United States Golf Association joined together in an effort to make the game universal and played under essentially the same set of rules, although many clubs have their own set of local rules. The rules of golf are very strict and stringent, sometimes bordering on the bizarre and, dare I say, they often sound stupid. That's the way it is and probably one of the reasons why the game has managed to keep its integrity intact for so many years.

Both these organisations are committed to promoting and developing the game, and the R&A have donated hundreds of thousands of pounds to various golf clubs and organisations throughout the world in an effort to 'keep things going'. Most of their funding comes from receipts from the Open Championship and its worldwide television rights; that, alongside all the other bits of infrastructure, go towards creating the world's most international golf championship. Then there is the Professional Golfers' Association (PGA) founded in 1901. This was put in place to guide and look after the interests of players who turn professional and attempt to earn their living through the game. Allied to that, you now have organisations looking after the needs of women who play the game professionally. Over the last few years we have seen a number of women take on the role of club professional and they have done excellent work, something that was unheard of thirty or forty years ago. Beverley Lewis became the first woman to be elected Captain of the Professional Golfers' Association, not quite as important as Lady Thatcher in her day but a huge step forward, not only for women's golf but the evolution of the game.

In my library I have one of the earliest, if not the earliest, copies of *The Golfer's Handbook*. In 1909 it was called *Who's Who in Golf*. It gives a list of members of golf clubs, and if they had managed to do anything outstanding it was recorded. The Open Championship that year was won by J. H. Taylor with a fine four-round score of 295. (Just think, seven over fours, which, on a wild day, would be considered pretty good today, even with all our modern equipment.) For those of you who may be interested in buying a copy of the R&A *Golfer's Handbook* (it's rather like cricket's *Wisden*), it's available by email from *golfmailing@macmillan.co.uk*, or you could write to Pan Macmillan, 20 New Wharf Road, London N1 9RR. This book really is a worthwhile investment. It has so many stories to tell, perhaps not many from modern times because feats of long driving now are commonplace, but it is interesting to look back fifty years to see what was recorded and marvel at some of the strange antics golfers got up to. For example: 'Earl Balfour, Prime Minister of the Day, won the Parliamentary Golf Tournament in 1894 and again in 1897 and said, "The wit of man has never invented a pastime equal to golf for its healthful recreation, its pleasurable excitement and its never ending source of amusement."' Interesting words over a hundred years ago but you could perhaps on occasion change that last word to 'frustration', even 'anger'!

We accept that golf is either 9 or 18 holes but that wasn't always so, many of the earliest golf courses only had 6 holes, some 7, 13, even 15. Going back to that first Open Championship in 1860, the course only had 12 holes and they played three rounds to complete 36 holes. Why 36? I'm not sure who decreed that number, perhaps it was because three rounds fitted nicely into the day, and that's the way the Championship was played until 1891. The fact that golf is played over 18 holes was brought about almost by accident. Where? Well, St Andrews of course. Somehow the players of the day found that they played out and they came back, finding sharing the fairways and even the huge double greens most convenient. At first the course had 22 holes but it was later altered by the first keeper of the green, Old Tom Morris, to accommodate the now 1st and 18th holes, so 18 holes became the ideal number for a round of golf. When the Open was first played there in 1873 they simply played two rounds of 18 holes each to conform to the then 36-hole duration of the championship.

Over the years much betting went on, which still happens to some degree today. I well remember Tony Jacklin, then the Open champion, driving a ball off the roof of the Savoy Hotel in London in an attempt to drive across the River Thames. I do believe the great American, Walter Hagen, had attempted this in the late 1920s and I'm sure others have tried. As long ago as 1798 two Scottish players attempted to drive over the spire of St Giles Cathedral in Edinburgh. They were allowed half a dozen shots each and managed to get a ball over the top, which meant over 160 feet. We are not told whether they hit any unwary pedestrians on landing! Remember, these early feats were all done with feathery golf balls, which weighed but a fraction of the 1.6 ounces they use today. There were a number of occasions when spectators interfered with play, much to the chagrin or those involved. Betting became fierce and watching particular favourites getting into trouble caused balls to be kicked back into play, which brought about many a bout of fisticuffs!

My father, Percy, was involved in an interesting situation in the Ryder Cup at Southport and Ainsdale Golf Club in 1937. He was playing Gene Sarazen and was on the par-three 15th. Father played a good tee shot, but the American's ball was well off-line and landed in the lap of a female spectator, who jumped up, flicking the ball from her skirt on to the green. It ended close to the hole, leaving a stymie – Sarazen got a two against father's three and Sarazen went on to win the match by one hole!

There are situations where golf balls have killed animals and fish, all sorts of freak accidents, players struck by lightning, one-armed, legless and ambidextrous players, cross-country matches, freak matches letting people do weird and wonderful things. Harry Dearth played a round at Bushy Hall wearing a suit of armour. And how about this – just before the start of the First World War, a gentleman called J. Farrar made a bet he would go round the Royston Golf Club in Hertfordshire in under a hundred strokes, equipped in full infantry marching order. He went round in 94 at odds of 10 to 1. Well done, what a man!

Here's another that caught my eye, simply because I played golf with A. J. (Bill) Young when I was a very young man and assistant to my father at Ferndown Golf Club. He was attached to the Sonning Golf Club on the outskirts of Reading. A certain Captain Pennington challenged Bill to a game of golf from the air – yes, from the air! The captain followed the course and dropped balls on to the greens – sounds simple, but the golf balls themselves were covered in cloth to make sure they didn't bounce away once they hit the ground. The gallant captain got round the course in forty minutes taking just twenty-nine strokes, whereas Bill took two hours and went round 18 holes in 68! Who was it who said all golfers are barmy? I'm not too sure what the rules of play were or, indeed, who claimed victory.

A player backed himself to go round a course in 200 throws and won his bet! For a wager some eccentrics have played using only a shovel, a rake, a baseball bat. Lee Trevino and Hedley Muscroft were both dab hands at hitting the ball with a Coca-Cola bottle. In the United States the Blind Golfers' Association was formed in 1946. Now it has branches in pretty well every golfing country in the world.

It was fashionable for some time to have Challenge matches – professionals from around the world gathered to play each other, there was usually a rich sponsor and big money was involved. In 1926 Walter Hagen and Abe Mitchell played a 72-hole match, 36 at Wentworth and 36 at St George's Hill. The stake was £1,000, a veritable fortune. Hagen was four down at one time, but recovered to win the match by 2 and 1. Although I don't remember being there, I am assured I was when A.D. 'Bobby' Locke and Sid Brews of South Africa challenged Reggie Whitcombe, who was the Open champion that year, and Henry Cotton to a £500 a side match, a total stake of £1,000, over 72 holes, the match a fourball. I've no idea why my father, Percy, was there but that's where he was in July 1938; I was seven! It was a very good battle with the South Africans installed as favourites, but it wasn't to be, the English pair won by 2 and 1. Thousands of spectators watched the last round, which was a huge success long before the days of television.

Gambling was getting a foothold a hundred years ago. J. H. Taylor, Harry Vardon, James Braid, Alex Herd, Alan Robertson, Old Tom Morris and the brothers Gunn were all involved in matches set up by the gentlemen of the day to see whether their professional could beat old so-and-so's pro down the road. Various sweeps were set up and big money was involved, a phenomenon that went on right through the 1960s and early '70s and was particularly prevalent when big pro-ams were being played and there was a dinner the night before when players were 'auctioned off'. I wouldn't be surprised if these activities still continue.

Play in our Open Championship has brought many disastrous scores to the forefront. Many years ago at the Troon (now Royal Troon) club, the German amateur, Herman Tissies, took 15 at the 120-yard 8th hole, the Postage Stamp. In and out of the bunkers he went, and eventually when he got on the green he three-putted; somehow he managed to get round in 92. Quite a feat!

The weather played a huge part in the 1938 Open Championship at Royal St George's in Kent; the golf traders' exhibition tent, the largest marquee ever erected at that time, was torn to shreds by the gale. Golf balls were blown off the greens, and a local pilot said he'd spotted cucumber sandwiches at 3,000 feet.

One score we tend to overlook is that of James Braid, who won the Open Championship at Prestwick in 1908 with a score of 291, which was then the lowest aggregate ever established at the championship over four rounds. The term 'par' had not been thought of, so play was worked out in level fours; most golf courses were 36 out and 36 back, so a four-round total was 288, which, under trying conditions, is still a good score even with today's equipment. But Braid, with the equipment of the day, was only three over fours, truly remarkable! The Postage Stamp at Troon is not perhaps as infamous as the Road Hole at St Andrews but then St Andrews is shown far more often on television than the Postage Stamp, and to say the Road Hole (the 17th) has taken its toll over the years would be an understatement! Even 11s, 12s and 13s were not uncommon and in recent times we've seen classy players taking umpteen shots to get out of the bunkers dotted around the Old Course. The reverse is also true and some lucky folk have scored immensely well. There have been scores of 58 recorded on 18-hole courses; obviously they are short but still require greens to be found and putts to be holed. Scores of 59 were regularly made on short courses, and by that I mean between 4,800 and 5,600 yards. Charlie Whitcombe, one of the three famous brothers, went round his own course, Crews Hill in North London, in 1937 in 59 shots, finishing with a run of seven 3s in a row. Over recent years a score of 60 is the dream of many top players. Indeed, one or two have broken that barrier, but if you work things out mathematically you could do much better.

Let us assume you have a course with four short holes and fourteen others. If you reach every hole in the allotted one or two shots, that's thirty-two; then have eighteen putts, your score adds up to 50! The list of strange situations goes on and on. Play abandoned because of rain, thunderstorms, lightning, snow, fog, the odd war, or a strike. Matches played in the dark. Feats of endurance. Many of these rounds have been played for charity – eight, ten, twelve, fourteen rounds in a day. More recently, when the wondrous aircraft Concorde was in operation, matches were organised that took players from Europe to America and across country so they played three or four rounds – in different 'worlds'. Long driving records are meaningless for a variety of reasons, not least because of the improved quality of golf balls, fairways being cut tighter, run on the ball, etc. – 260 yards years ago was a great feat – now 350 yards is almost commonplace.

A certain Miss Poppy Wingate was the assistant professional at the Temple Newsam Golf Club on the outskirts of Leeds while my father was professional there for a couple of years in the mid-thirties. It caused quite a stir when she turned up to play in the Leeds Cup, a professional tournament in 1933! The great Babe Zaharias, who won athletics gold medals at the 1932 Olympics, then turned to golf, was a truly remarkable athlete. She competed with the men on golf courses in the years just after the Second World War. This is not so unusual today. We've had Michelle Wie attempting to compete with the men and, indeed, Annika Sorenstam playing as recently as 2006 in the Skins Game, but neither was able to make the men tremble in their passing.

There have been holes halved in one, successive holes in one, holing out twice in the same round, the longest hole in one, the list continues.

Speaking of holes in one, it's a fact that some of the best players, the most accurate strikers, have had very few. Harry Vardon only had one hole in one – rather like Seve Ballesteros and my father, Percy Alliss, a most accurate player, who both achieved but a single hole in one. The American Art Wall, a good player, and winner of numerous tournaments in America, including the Masters, also a member of a couple of Ryder Cup teams, had over forty holes in one, which caused Jimmy Demaret, one of the great players of the day and renowned wag, to remark, 'He plays a lot of his golf in west Texas where dust storms are always happening; they say he's always first on to the green at the short holes!' I don't know what on earth he was suggesting, but forty holes in one – wow! Albert Chevalier, a professional from Lancashire, certainly had well over twenty. Of course, the hole has to be receptive, a bit of a 'bowl' where, when the flag's in a certain position, it rather 'gathers' than 'fends off', but still the shot has to be played and verified.

The odds against holing in one are considerable, although quite a number have been done in tournament play over the years. It used to be a feature to have a big prize for a hole in one, sometimes larger than the total prize fund. In the mid-sixties we were playing in the Esso Round Robin Tournament on the High Course at Moor Park near Watford. On offer was a prize of £10,000 for a hole in one at the 18th, a shortish par-three, slightly downhill. The South African Harold Henning holed in one, much to the delight of two or three of his friends who all thought they were splitting the proceeds. Whether or not this was so, someone was happy!

Years ago they had a competition in the United States to see how many shots it would take to get a hole in one. They chose a hole of 130 yards, had over 200 professionals taking part, each given five balls, well over a thousand attempts, and nobody got closer than a couple of feet, which just shows what a fluke it is to pop the ball into a hole $4\frac{1}{4}$ inches in diameter.

It is interesting to look back and see what constituted slow play. In 1938 the big match between Henry Cotton and Reggie Whitcombe, Bobby Locke and Sid Brews at Walton

Heath drew 5,000 spectators. The first round took three hours and forty minutes, the second four hours and fifteen minutes. It was considered an outrage. Today both times would be more than acceptable for a fourball; nowadays fourball Ryder Cup matches take over five hours and in the World Cup, a fourball medal and other such competitions, it's not unusual for rounds to take over six hours.

One final note on slow play. In 1950 the Amateur Championship was played at St Andrews, and the final was between two Americans, Frank Stranahan and Dick Chapman. The first 9 holes of the morning round took one hour and fifty minutes. A message was sent to the referee, Colonel Hezlet, the golfing patriarch from Royal Portrush, who warned that the second round would be started at the scheduled time. This increased the pace of play slightly and the round was finished in three hours and forty minutes, which at that time was the slowest final round in the championship's history. Will those days ever return? Sadly I doubt it.

Gate money has some interesting statistics. In 1892 a match between Doug White and Douglas Roland was played at Chesterfield Park in Cambridgeshire. It was the first time there was a charge to watch golf. In 1905 the St Anne's International Foursomes were played and spectators paid two shillings and sixpence each ($12\frac{1}{2}$ p in today's money) for the privilege. After 1906 it became more the norm and for the first time money was paid to watch the Amateur Championship. The year was 1926. It was played at Muirfield on the east side of Edinburgh, the take for the week was just under £1,000, which worked out at 9,000 people for the week or over 1,500 per day. In 1925 for the first time gate money was charged to watch the Boys. The US Open, played at Oakland Hills in 1951 raked in over US$110,000, a record amount at that time; today it runs into many millions.

Special rules were introduced to compensate for the war

years, 1939–45. Players were asked to collect bomb and shell splinters from the fairways to save causing damage to the mowers. If there was any gunfire or bombing whilst playing, competitors could take cover without penalty for delaying play. Unexploded bombs were marked by red and white flags, placed at reasonably safe distances from the bombs, but there was no guarantee of life or limb! Shell and bomb splinters on the greens could be removed without penalty, the same on fairways or in bunkers; there should be no penalty if the ball was moved during shrapnel clearance. A ball lying in any crater might be lifted and dropped nearer the hole with no penalty; and I love this one: 'A player whose stroke is affected by simultaneous explosion of a bomb, a shell or by machine gun fire, may play another ball from the same spot. Penalty one stroke.' How cruel!

But mostly golfers are survivors. Witness long-lived Canadian golfer Arthur Thomson, who equalled his age when he was 103, on a course measuring over 6,000 yards. Nathaniel Vickers, George Miller and a number of other players have reached that time in life when a telegram comes from the Queen sending congratulations for having lived a hundred summers and being still able to enjoy one of the most extraordinary, painful, pleasurable, miserable, delightful pastimes ever invented by man.

TIMETABLE OF THE RULES OF THE GAME

1744 The first time a code of rules was put together, it was known as the 13 Articles. It was produced by the Honourable Company of Edinburgh Golfers. Ten years later the R&A recorded their own rules in the minutes.

1812 The first time the rules of golf referred to bunkers and the putting green.

1842   It was decided for the first time that 18 holes were 'a match'.

1875   You could have the flagstick attended.

1882   The R&A defined the size of hole as 4 inches in diameter, lined with iron. It was changed four years later, which defined the hole as 4 inches in diameter and 6 inches deep. In 1889 the R&A revised their thinking and the hole became $4\frac{1}{4}$ inches in diameter and at least 4 inches deep; that remains in place to this very day.

1897   The year my father was born, the Royal & Ancient Golf Club is recognised as the game's Governing Body for the Rules of Golf.

1909   New legislature appeared on the limits and shape that clubs should take.

1920   It was agreed between Britain and the United States that a golf ball should be no greater than 1.62 ounces in weight and not less than 1.62 inches in diameter.

1929   Steel shafts appeared.

1939   The maximum number of clubs that could be carried became fourteen. Up to that time you could have as many clubs as your caddie could carry. Why? Well, wooden shafts broke with great regularity, so you needed a few spares standing by.

1952   As recently as then the R&A and the USGA established a unified code of rules.

1960   Machines for measuring distances were banned from use in competitive play.

1984   The ball no longer had to be dropped over the shoulder, which had made for many weird contortions; now the rule was that you simply had to stretch your arm out shoulder high and drop, very sensible, and I've no idea why it wasn't thought of much earlier. Thank you, Grant Spaeth, the man responsible for that idea, then a member of the USGA and various other committees.

1990 The American-size ball, 1.68 inches, became the only legal ball, bringing an end to the British-size 1.62 ball.

IMPORTANT DATES AND HAPPENINGS IN THE WORLD OF GOLF

Particularly the Open Championship and the R&A

1964 The first grandstands were erected at Open Championships.

1966 The first live coverage of the Open Championship was beamed into America, presented by the ABC Television Company, with whom I had a very happy working association for more than thirty years.

1966 It wasn't until then that the championship was played over four days. The venue? Muirfield.

1974 The bigger size ball, the 1.68-inch, became compulsory in the Open Championship.

1980 The championship finished on a Sunday for the first time, again played at Muirfield.

1985 The R&A changed the playoff arrangements for the Open Championship. Instead of 36 and 18 holes, which had been the previous arrangements over the past hundred years, it was now decided there would be a 4-hole playoff; the player with the lowest score at the end would be the champion. It wasn't universally received with acclamation, and not at all by the United States Golf Association. They insist on an 18-hole playoff the following day, which causes much disruption, but that's the way they like it.

1990   The American 1.68-inch golf ball became the only legal
       ball in the world of golf.
2004   This year saw the celebration of the Royal and Ancient's
       250th anniversary.

As recently as 2007 the Old Course at St Andrews was used for
the first time, firstly for the Women's British Championship and
in 2008 for the Curtis Cup, where the amateurs of Great
Britain and Ireland take on the might of America.

4

HOW TO START GOLF

'The harder I work, the luckier I get.'
GARY PLAYER

There are many reasons why people take up golf, particularly in middle age. Many have been active in other sports but the time comes when the body says enough is enough. The options then for an alternative outdoor sport for an energetic person, after their hockey, rugby, football, tennis days have come to an end, aren't all that many, so the thought of golf can loom quite large.

If you have decided to give golf a go, I urge you first to sit down and give it some thought. After all, there are many things you have done or are doing in your life that you've taken ages to ponder, whether it be buying a new car, redecorating the house, getting a new sofa, rejigging the kitchen, deciding where to go on holiday, or investing in some new clothes – I bet you've devoted a bit of time to them! But, you know, a lot of people just start golf on a whim. Their initial introduction is likely to be via a friend, and if they show any aptitude someone, out of the kindness of their heart, gives/lends/sells them a few clubs that in 90 per cent of cases are totally wrong for their skill or physique. Perhaps some of these words will appear elementary or boring to certain readers. I hope it's neither, but do get a piece of paper and make some headings. Not sure what to put down? Well, here are a few starters for you.

A number of people are put off the game of golf by the feeling that it's going to cost them a lot of money from day one. This is not true. The best place to start is probably at a local driving range. Ask to see the head professional. Most, if not all, these driving ranges have PGA (Professional Golfers Association) approved professionals on duty. Make an appointment to see one – remember you may have to book because he could be busy. He will certainly allocate you fifteen or twenty minutes of his time, which, in the majority of occasions, pros are happy to give free. I doubt if any have ever charged for a short consultation with someone who's about to start the game of golf. Ask his advice. He will be in a position to lend you some clubs if you decide to take a short course of lessons. If, for example, you book six lessons pretty close together, at the end of that time both he and you will know whether or not you have any aptitude and, indeed, could make, if not rapid, certainly steady progress.

Find out if there are any group classes in your area. This is a very good way to start, as long as the numbers aren't too great and the teachers not spread too thinly. Learning with a group can give you confidence, which in all sports is one of the biggest ingredients.

If you don't have a driving range close to home, usually there's a golf club, where you shouldn't be put off by the 'private members only' sign on the door. Find the pro shop and, again, go in and tell the pro what you're thinking of doing and ask if he can help. How can he help? I think the early stages of taking up golf are very important. Of course, there have always been players who proudly boast they never had a lesson in their life and they play to a relatively low handicap – 6, 8, 10, but they might have been better than that with just a few small changes to the swing, which would have made the game that little bit easier.

Once you've had your half a dozen lessons and like the thought of going further, it could be time to invest in some clubs. There are thousands of sets of second-hand clubs on the market at very reasonable prices. The professional will advise you which type of club you should look for. I would suggest you buy no more than ten clubs to start with, more than sufficient to set you on your way. By now you will have discovered whether your hands blister. If you are a right-handed player, blistering, particularly on the left hand, is very prevalent, so you may need to wear a glove on your left hand. The idea of this is to give you a firmer grip that stops your hands sliding about; if your hands move it causes friction and thereby you get blisters. You will need a pair of golf shoes and, although they are not cheap, they are not a lot more expensive than a decent pair of trainers. Trainers are not the ideal footwear, although quite usable during the dry summer months, but at other times you will need something with some form of studded sole and heel to give you a grip.

As you continue there's a whole lot of things you will find on offer in the pro shop, or wherever your feet and eyes take you – umbrellas, hats, waterproof jacket and trousers, sweaters, a myriad of goodies.

Golf is recognised as being a difficult game, and so a complete set of clubs comprises as many as fourteen of them, each to do a specific job. Because of the variance in loft and lies, each club hits the ball a different distance. The driver has the longest shaft and usually the straightest face and hits the ball the farthest. At the other end, a club with a shortish shaft and the most loft – usually up to 60 degrees – is for the short shots which modern golfers play so well. Then, of course, there are a multitude of putters of all shapes and sizes, all promising to work their magic.

If you are going to attempt to progress properly, it's going to cost you some money but not a fortune. And again remember how you set about the other accomplishments in your life, whether learning to play the piano or some other musical instrument, dancing, singing, cooking, spinning, any lessons at all in the world of sport, and, of course, driving a car. They all needed working on for you to succeed.

Remember also that there are different under-foot conditions that prevail in golf, the texture of the grass, the length of it, the speed of the greens, the texture of sand in the bunkers, the roll on the green, learning to read the line, this is all before you start on the complexity of the rules, which can sound monstrously difficult. But having got this out of the way, my purpose is to encourage you and not to put you off. I do assure you, if you're going to join our happy band of brothers, that there are no more than a dozen rules you need to learn by heart; they will give you the nucleus of the game and get you out of many a scrape, most times working in your favour.

Oh, and by the way, in other games like tennis and cricket players run for shelter as soon as it starts to rain; golfers, particularly those in competitive play, continue until the course is unplayable, until the greens are covered with water or the wind so fierce the ball blows away under its own volition! I've played on many days like that and the thought often crossed my mind, 'Why haven't I taken up cricket or tennis?' But then those tennis players, particularly the modern ones, rush all over the world and have the most amazing metabolisms; their fitness levels are now quite extraordinary –

or perhaps it's all down to the bananas they eat, I often wonder if they contain some magic formula!

You may, of course, live near some open ground, and although you must be very careful when hitting a golf ball not to endanger life or limb, it is possible, on many occasions, to go somewhere with a few golf balls in your pocket, an eight- or nine-iron, and just walk along the open way with the old dog for company, do a bit of chipping and putting, getting the feeling of the ball going off the club face.

You may have to make some sacrifices. If you really become keen the summer months can be used to your advantage. Being an early riser myself, I know the delights of a summer's morning long before many have stirred, the clean air and the bird song for company. I'm talking about any time after 5.30 a.m. Does that horrify you? Well don't let it because once you get into that routine you've no idea how enjoyable it will become.

You cannot learn about golf and become even reasonably proficient if you're not prepared to put in a little bit of practice time. Unfortunately most people want a magic fix. They would love to go to their professional and get either a magic club or a mystical pill that will do the trick but, sadly, there's no easy answer. It's like going on a diet. Michael Winner, the film-maker and bon viveur, brought out a wonderful book called *The Fat Pig's Diet*, and at the end of it all – 231 pages in fact – it said, 'Be disciplined and eat less!'

If you start out from day one with a proper plan, seeking good knowledge along the way, many things will drop into place more easily. The thing is, don't rush. If you're thinking of taking up the game, find a period of perhaps two or three weeks when you can fit those half a dozen lessons in fairly close together; it's not much good having one every month, or even every two weeks, as you tend to forget what you learnt in the first lesson. One a day for a period would be pretty good if you can do it – hotels and resorts offer beginner's packages, if you want to combine it with a holiday. I would say, that for an initial outlay of about £250 and the right tutor, you should be able to get some idea as to whether the game of golf suits you, whether you would enjoy it, whether it fits your temperament, your rhythm of life.

> *'In Switzerland I was reading one of my own instruction books and realised I was too open at address. How easy it is to forget the fundamentals of this game.'*
> SEVE BALLESTEROS, to the press at the 1989 European Masters

It's an interesting fact that if you give practically anyone a simple walking stick and ask them to hit a fir cone or a pebble, they will do it either one- or two-handed but make a passable swing at the object. The moment they have a golf club in their hands, whether because they've seen too many pictures or watched too much television, they get themselves into the most bizarre positions, with a total lack of rhythm. I've always used my hands a lot in my swing, the hands control the club head. If you really give it a good waggle and think in terms of a table tennis shot or a forehand drive at tennis, you get some idea how the arm should go through the ball to the target.

My father, Percy, a great player in his day and a first-class teacher, had a theory that you must get as many things as possible right before you take the club away from the ball. These were wise words because the actual swing is over in a split second and it is virtually impossible to correct anything once it has actually begun. That means paying attention to the following: the grip, with both hands comfortably on the club, how you stand to the ball, your stance, posture and the angle of the spine, the position of the ball, aiming correctly, knees flexed 50/50, weight distributed nice and evenly – all of a sudden you are beginning to look as if you know what you're doing!

The Grip

The only contact you have in golf is through your hands. The great thing is to get the hands to work together. Up until the mid-sixties there were several leading professionals with eccentric grips and swings who somehow managed to get the clubhead back to the ball, were good chippers and putters and could make a living, but now most players look comfortable; this should be your aim. Find the grip that's most comfortable for you and stick with it.

There are basically three grips used today and no doubt, with a little bit of practice, one of them will suit you. When the game began the grips on the clubs were very thick, players gripped the club very crudely, and it wasn't until the early 1900s that Harry Vardon discovered a revolutionary way of gripping the club – putting the little finger of the right hand over or between the index finger of the left hand. I must remind you that this tuition is for right-handed players, the reverse would be the case if you are left-handed, i.e. the little finger of the left hand would be over the index finger of the right.

The interlocking grip, which has attained a tremendous amount of popularity over the last twenty years or so, and is used by some of the world's very finest players, shows us that the little finger of both hands are locked together.

The final grip is known as the baseball grip, where no fingers overlap or interlock but are together.

You will notice from the illustrations that the hands look comfortable on the shaft and work together as a unit; golf is a two-handed game and that thought should be constantly in your mind, particularly if you are a beginner. I am often asked how tightly a golf club should be held. The answer is not tightly at all – but firmly. Your grip must be firm enough for the club not to move in your hands at any point in the swing.

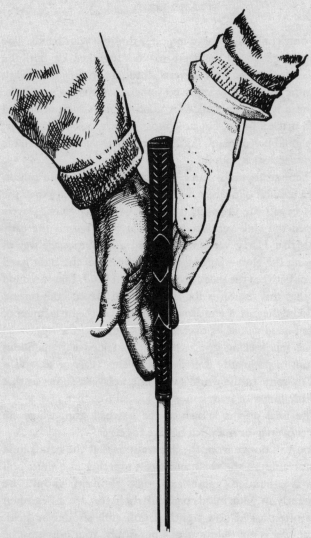

The first step in gripping the
club is almost like clapping
your hands

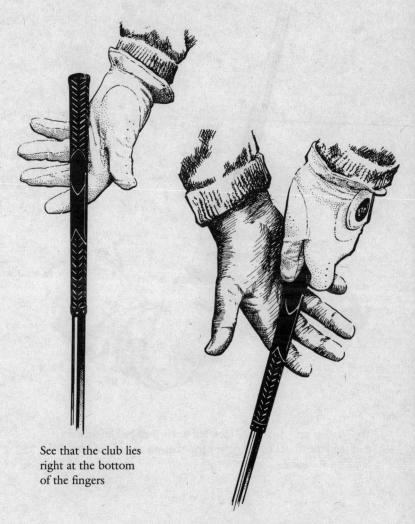

See that the club lies
right at the bottom
of the fingers

Note that the right-hand
grip is also entirely at the
base of the fingers

The Vardon grip is virtually identical to the baseball grip except that the little finger of the right hand rests on top of the first finger of the left

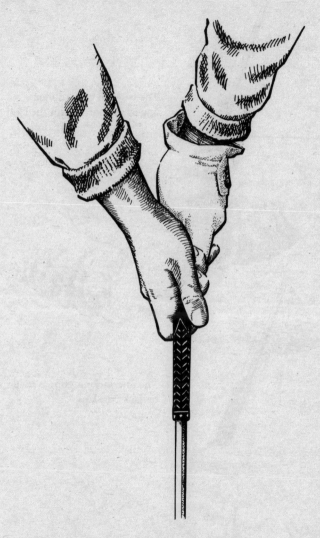

The perfect Vardon grip

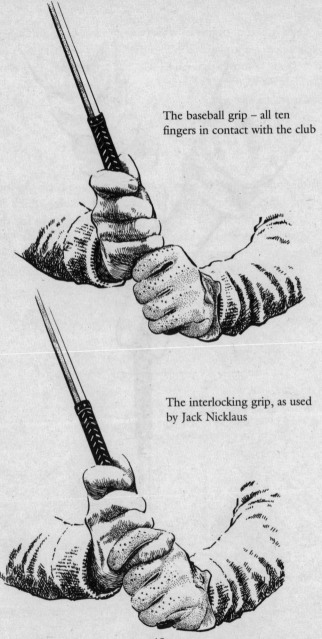

The baseball grip – all ten
fingers in contact with the club

The interlocking grip, as used
by Jack Nicklaus

Gripping too tightly is a very common fault and often occurs because a player is nervous. The results make a good golf swing almost impossible as you can't swish the arms through freely and it becomes more of a heave with the body rather than a swing.

THE STANCE

Posture and learning to stand to the ball are not as easy as you might think. The great thing is to be comfortable – think of everything being 50/50 – weight distribution, more or less on the balls of your feet (imagine a clock face with your feet pointing at five minutes to one), arms and club pretty well in a straight line back from the ball to your shoulder, the head sitting in a nice natural position, looking at the ball with both eyes, with your chin neither tilted up nor down.

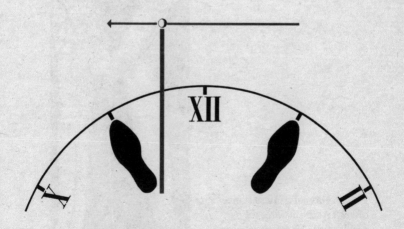

The 'five to one' foot position

The old cliché is that the feet should be the same width as the shoulders and there is little wrong with this except that people have the oddest notions about how wide their shoulders are. Ian Marchbank, who was the professional at Gleneagles, once gave me a good tip which is easy for the beginner to grasp. 'Take your natural walking stride,' he advised, 'then stop and just swivel around square to an imaginary ball. It's your natural stride length and that's how you will be best balanced because it's what your body is used to.'

The easy-looking Alliss stance of yesteryear showing the width of the stance in relation to the shoulders

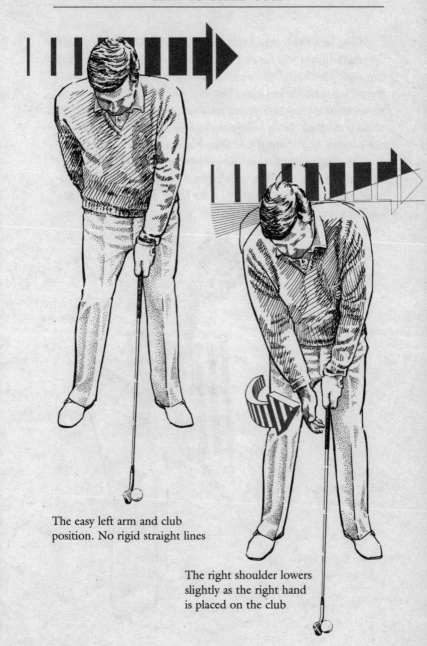

The easy left arm and club
position. No rigid straight lines

The right shoulder lowers
slightly as the right hand
is placed on the club

Many beginners stand too far away from the ball and end up reaching out too far or too crouched. Others have the ball too close and have little room to swing the club. Where is the happy medium? Stand erect but not too stiff, flex both knees a couple of inches as if sitting on a stool just below the height of your bottom. Now hold the club and left arm out towards the ground in a straight line (but without the arm being stiff) until the blade lies flat on the ground and just inside the line of your left heel. That is the distance away from the ball that suits your height and length of arm. Make sure your shoulders and hips are still square to the target.

Note the angle of club and wrist – the wrist is not too low or arched too high

As in any ball game, the ball must be watched at least until impact. Look at it with both eyes, but *don't* look at the top. You are going to be trying to get the clubhead into the *back* of the ball. Looking at the top is no help at all. You want to have the feeling of your swing coming in at the back and through the ball on the same line.

THE SWING

The takeaway

This is, roughly, the first couple of feet of the backswing. It should begin with shoulders, hips, arms and hands moving in unison, nothing leading and nothing lagging behind. Keep the clubhead almost brushing the ground and travelling straight back. We must avoid either lifting the club or bringing it sharply inwards.

Nearing the top

Simply continue swinging the club back with hands and arms while your shoulders and back turn away from the ball until your back is square to the target. You must at no point lift the club into any position. The golf swing is a turning, swinging movement. As long as you don't let your wrists break too early, it really doesn't matter, but the later the better. This helps the rest of the body to turn to the top of the back swing.

The top of the swing

This differs with each person. Golf can be played with very different lengths of backswing. Doug Sanders did not get the club up much above his shoulders, while others get beyond the horizontal, most notably John Daly. The two vital elements, if we are to make a swing of any real power, are a full turn of the shoulders and getting the hands well away from the ball, as far as you can comfortably manage and certainly above shoulder height.

Easy position at the top of the backswing. Club pointing to the target. Left knee looking down on the right foot

Beginning the downswing

So far, the golf swing I have been teaching you has been a matter of first getting the stationary bits right and then swinging the clubhead back fairly slowly and in a relaxed way. Things are now about to speed up and troubles often start when the backswing is completed and the golfer begins to swing back to the ball. It is here that players show their anxiety. Psychologically, they may be afraid of making a bad shot or of missing the ball. There comes a sudden jerk as they try to get the whole thing over with. But we should be in no hurry.

We want no sudden jerk or heave of the shoulders; the arms should swing down and through the back of the ball with the feeling of hitting it *forward*. As you begin that movement, you can feel the muscles of your left side doing most of the work, pulling the clubhead into the hitting area. Your hips will take care of themselves, turning naturally until square to the target by the time you hit the ball. Your shoulders will also turn naturally, but you will do better if you feel they are square to the ball at the point of contact. If you let them turn away too soon, the path of your swing will be from right to left and you will cut across the ball, losing both distance and direction. If your clubface is closed as you strike the ball, it will fly straight left; if square or open, it will curl weakly away to the right.

In the hitting area

What happens in the hitting area is mostly the result of what has gone before, swinging back and beginning the downswing in the way I have described. But what, you may ask, about the hands? They come in late on in the swing, as you approach the ball, providing the final acceleration. Remember, I am saying 'final'. Use them too early and you will push the clubhead in front of your hands and that pulling movement will be gone.

But that's by no means the worst effect. Think back to how you began the backswing. You set the club to aim precisely at your target. That is the position that the whole swing aims to reach once again at the moment of impact between clubhead and ball. But it is impossible if the hands take over too early and *throw* the clubhead at the ball. Allowing the head of the club to meet the ball with the hands behind rather than leading is the single most common fault amongst relatively poor golfers.

However, it is rather difficult for the golfer to know when he's developed this fault because this is the high-speed area of the swing. We can't see what's happening. But most of you, perhaps all, should be able to feel that pulling movement all the time until after the ball has been struck.

If not, it's easy to observe the results you will achieve when you let the clubhead get in advance of the hands. Topped or mishits will be more frequent, but above all there will be little consistency. The ball will fly to right or left equally unpredictably because in the split-second timing of the hitting area, with very narrow margins for error, the clubhead will not reach the ball in the same position twice running.

Swing speed

For the downswing, all players, when hitting more or less full out, want as much acceleration as they can generate and control. You'll soon learn just what you can control and what you can't.

The speed of the backswing, however, is very much an individual matter. Top professionals, for example, vary a very great deal. People used to say that Dai Rees swung the club back as fast as down – an exaggeration, of course, but it was a quicker movement than the eye could follow. Another contemporary of his, former US Open champion Dr Cary Middlecoff, swung the club back extremely slowly and then came to a dead halt at the top. He felt the pause enabled him to make a smooth and balanced transition from the backwards to the downwards movement. Though Middlecoff was a prodigious tournament winner, I don't recommend his technique for lesser mortals. With that kind of pause, you will probably lose all rhythm – and even get stuck up there! Stranger things have been known.

For a good contrast, we need look no further than Jack Nicklaus and Tom Watson. Nicklaus was slow, Watson fast. As models, both are probably a little too extreme; something in between is required.

What you must aim at is a balanced rhythmic change of direction as you begin to move down to the ball again. There should be a fleeting moment when you feel nicely poised and in the right position to pour everything down towards the ball and beyond. You also need to feel your right wrist underneath the shaft and your left ready to lead the right.

Undoubtedly this is more easily achieved if your backswing is slow rather than fast. All of us have to resist the tendency to swing back more quickly when tension is at a height; it's often then that a golfer with a fast action comes to grief.

The follow-through

This is the part of the golf swing that matters not one jot. Once the clubhead has met the ball, you can fall flat on your face if you like. At the other extreme, the most elegant of statuesque finishes to the swing will gain you nothing at all. The ball is long gone, for better or worse. The follow-through is simply the result of what has gone before. How you finish is useful in highlighting faults – as I pointed out in discussing the right-sided heave at the ball – particularly after a cut shot. However, the perfect follow-through does not mean that a perfect shot has been played, only that you made a good swing which may well have not been on exactly the right path. I remember a photo caption which said: 'The poise of the follow-through is excellent. Unfortunately the ball only just missed my left kneecap.'

Leg action

In the backswing, the legs move in sympathy with the rest of the body. As you progress into your one-piece takeaway, your left knee should bend, more or less directly, towards the right foot, though this is quite a small movement, say about six inches and no more. The right leg moves far less, just a twisting movement as it follows your torso action, eventually resisting towards the end of the backswing. The leg will be fairly taut, but by no means stiff, when the hips have completed their movement. This is through about 45 degrees rather than the 90 degrees or more of the shoulders. The feet should tend to roll and the left heel can be allowed to leave the ground, though preferably not.

Broadly speaking, on the downswing the legs will take care of themselves. Certainly, for a beginner, I do not recommend you getting yourself involved in the theory you may come across about leg drive and how it increases distance. Severiano Ballesteros has played a round of golf in about level par on his knees. There is negligible extra distance to be gained from leg action. What is important is that the legs should follow the rest of the body and move away from and back into the ball smoothly and on the right path.

KEEPING YOUR EYE ON THE BALL

There are two particular points I want to make which apply to every stroke from drive to putt. Do not merely look at the ball. This means that you will probably just be aware of the top, whereas it is the back you are always trying to find. Throughout your backswing, the ball must remain in view. Notice particularly what happens at the top of the swing, for it is at this point your head may be pulled by the tug of shoulders on neck. If this happens to you, a trick worth trying is to set your head a little to the right before you start swinging, as Jack Nicklaus and many other players do. The head must be kept still, though unavoidably it slides a little right and then left during the two parts of the swing.

The other moment of danger comes when the player wants to see the results of his shot. As the brain works more quickly than the body, it is instinctive to think the ball has been struck before it has. If you aren't looking at the ball in that final instant, it matters little in theory, but other faults follow. After all, we do not lift just our eyes to follow the flight of a ball, but our head and shoulders as well. If this happens, there is no possibility at all of making good contact with the ball. All too often a topped shot is the result.

The old Ryder Cup player, Irishman Harry Bradshaw, drilled himself not to follow the run of the ball at all. Instead, he kept his head down and listened for the sound of the ball rattling into the hole. Try it. Of course, this does not do for long shots. Lost balls will result!

Through the green, then, I suggest that either you drill yourself to try to see the clubhead strike the ball (impossible, of course) or watch the back of the ball until your brain accepts that it has gone.

Listen for the swish

I have been telling you how the golf swing is a pulling, not a pushing or throwing, movement. If I haven't convinced you, I want you to try a simple little experiment. Make a smooth unhurried backswing and then give your all in a right-handed bash at the ball. Try that again, this time listening for the swish your club makes through the air. And again. Keep the fastest sounds you make in your mind and now go back to the swing where you have the feeling of pulling into the ball. It's a great deal faster. That feeling of strength in your right side is a bit of a cheat. You are using only about half your natural capability to accelerate the clubhead through the ball. If you pull with the left side, you bring all your capability into the swing. The right side has its say too – but late in the downswing, not near the beginning. When it actually comes into play is mostly a matter of letting nature take its course. It cannot be really deliberate because at that stage everything happens at such a high speed.

So far, I have been talking about the basic golf swing for all shots, irons as well as woods. There is very little difference in the swing whatever club you are using, but I want to discuss those differences, such as they are.

THE DRIVE

Although a ball positioned just inside the left heel is recommended, you may benefit by moving the ball forward an inch or two towards your left toe. Most golf shots are struck both forward and down. For the drive, however, a descending blow costs distance because a little more backspin is put on the ball. The shot may be impeccably straight (although it is apt to be a slice), but the result is a ball that flies higher than ideal and has very little run. Instead, the clubhead should come into the ball on a horizontal line (parallel to the ground), or just after it has reached the bottom of its arc and begins to rise on the upswing. There will be a little less backspin, resulting in less height and more roll. This is really the meaning of the old saying, 'Tee it high and let it fly.' When a player sets his ball high, he has the feeling that his club will go up at the ball. So place the ball a little farther forward and tee it up at whatever height gives you the feeling that you are striking through and very slightly up at the moment of impact. The actual height is a matter of personal choice and will result from trial and error.

And remember, your swing path must ensure that the clubhead is travelling along the target line when it reaches the hitting zone and the clubface is square to the target line. A ball with a lot of sidespin on it – a quick hook or slice – loses direction as well as length.

The imaginary view of the driver swinging the ball away on an upward path

FAIRWAY WOODS

Assuming that you have a good fairway lie, there are two ways of striking a fairway wood. One is to sweep the ball away clean, either without touching the turf or just brushing it. This gives the maximum distance. The other is to deliver a slightly descending blow with, naturally, a divot being taken. The latter is suitable when the ball is sitting low and a sweeping shot would be likely to result in your taking turf before hitting the ball or topping the shot. You will lose a little length, but this is usually less important for a fairway shot than for the drive. When playing with woods it is also possible to develop a punched wooden-club shot. This can be useful when playing from a divot mark or when the ball is well down in the grass.

When in the rough, don't be afraid of taking a wood, but do be sensible about it. It's sometimes possible to have a lie good enough for a driver, when kindly Providence has perched the ball, say, an inch above the ground. If the lie is not quite perfect, a fairway wood is better than a long-iron, which has to cut, rather than push, through the grass. If the ball is set well down, only a player with fast, strong hand action should consider using a long-iron. Think of Arnold Palmer. He lost the 1966 US Open when in a dominating position because he took long-irons from doubtful lies – and there's never been a more powerful man with a long-iron than Palmer.

When using a wood from a moderate lie in the rough, always choose the club with the smallest head for it will travel through the grass more easily. The four-wood will often be suitable and some players have a number five or an even more lofted club – a 'heaven seven' or even the 'divine nine'. These days there is also the rescue club, a hybrid of a long-iron faced club with the clubhead shape of a fairway wood. It is ideal for exactly these situations.

Do not strive for maximum length. Good contact with the ball from a controlled swing is what you are after.

If you decide the lie is not good enough to be worth risking a wood, you should then switch your choice to a fairly lofted iron, certainly no straighter in the face than a five-iron.

Fairway woods can also be used from fairway bunkers, but do be sensible. Ask yourself if you're an accurate enough striker for it to be worth the risk. If you take sand before the ball, you will get very little distance indeed and a topped shot will almost always remain in the bunker.

LONG-IRONS

As with a driver, many golfers feel that they have to hit the long-irons full out. This is a great mistake. (I am referring here to three-irons, since one- and two-irons are only advisable for the very low-handicap player.) Remember, all irons are supposed to be precision clubs. I advise you to hit, say, your three-iron no harder than you would a normal full shot with a seven- or eight-iron. If you feel the need to thrash away at the ball, you would be far better off playing a controlled wooden-club shot. I've seen handicap golfers in their thousands using an iron at long par-three holes when they have no real chance of reaching the green, except with a once-in-a-lifetime shot. The silly fellows don't like to take a wood because the hole is 'only' 190 yards – quite possibly the distance they get with their average drives.

Remember that the long-iron is the most difficult club in the bag to hit well. If you are a golfer who finds them difficult, a seven-wood might well be worth the purchase price. I have seen some club golfers' games transformed when they have acknowledged to themselves, sometimes as a result of growing older, that they cannot play long-irons effectively.

As well as for play to the greens, the long-irons are invaluable for tee shots to the fairway on those days when your driving is off. Remember also that on many fairly short par-fours a good architect will have put a premium on placement of the tee shot. To be in the right or left half of the fairway may well be far more important than being fifty yards farther on but on the 'wrong' side, with the approach menaced by rough and bunkers or the flag set in a difficult position.

You must, however, devote a lot of time to practice. Undeniably, a long-iron requires more skill and experience than, say, a fairway wood, but the rewards are greater.

MID-IRONS

Basically these are the clubs numbered four to seven, the easiest to use. You may meet problems with other irons, either because of lack of loft or because of too much loft for your particular swing faults. This problem should not occur with the mid-irons; whatever your faults, you should be able to get the ball in the air and not sky your shots too much.

Just use your normal golf swing and, once again, don't hit full out. There are no special prizes for getting on to the green with a seven-iron when others are using a five. It's simply where the ball finished that counts.

I would also suggest that you become particularly friendly with your five-iron. It will move the ball a fair distance and can come in very useful for keeping the ball in play when you are horribly off form, as happens to all of us.

THE APPROACH CLUBS

Here I am mainly talking about the eight, the nine, the pitching wedge and the sand iron, when you are using a full swing. The main difficulties with these clubs come from variable length. On the one hand, there are golfers who hit all of them rather too high and, on the other, those who hit them too low. In the first case this is usually caused by the hands being behind the clubhead, thus increasing the clubhead loft; in the second, the hands are too far ahead, which, of course, has the reverse result. And check your ball position, which can affect either case a great deal. If this is satisfactory, the fault must be in your hands in relation to clubhead position. This is far less easy to check. On the practice ground try to get the feel of your position at the point of impact. Better still, try to get someone to film you with a video camera or even a mobile phone.

You may be asking why very high or very low shots should be avoided. The main reason is that either the pattern of play produces too great a variety of distance, especially with the pitching wedge and the sand iron, where the control of distance means the difference between being up to the flag, short of the green or well through the green.

Let me give you an example. I have heard club golfers – and professionals as well for that matter – boast that they can hit a sand wedge 120 yards. If true, all this means is that they are losing a great proportion of the stopping power of the club. They are hitting the ball an exceptional distance, but the flight is low, perhaps with some hook on the ball. The obvious result is that the ball will run on farther than required. The reverse is also unhelpful. With very high shots, you will begin to hit harder in order to get extra distance, whereas it is precision and control that are desperately wanted – and that's the name of this part of the golf game.

Move the ball back in the stance if you are hitting too high, forward if too low. You can also vary the position of your hands on the grip. Holding the club right at the top of the shaft tends to produce high shots. The lower down you grip the club, the lower the ball will fly.

Above all, remember that these are precision clubs. It doesn't matter in the least which club you use or how far you hit it. What matters is how close to the flag your ball finishes.

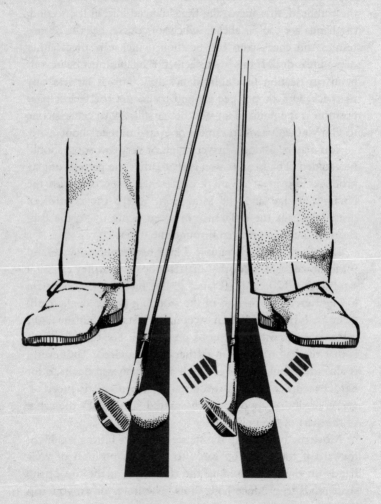

Variations in ball position for iron play, but beware of exaggeration

PUTTING

It's not just a game within a game, but two, perhaps even three, games in one. From, let's say, twenty yards you are trying to get the ball near the hole; from a few strides the aim is to leave your ball on the lip or at the bottom of the hole; our third category is holing out in the range where it is really a bit shameful to miss – those two-to-four-footers, or even less.

Of course, the putting stroke is exactly the same for all these distances, though the mental attitude is not. From a long distance, you ought to be trying to get the feel of the yards to be covered into your finger and arm muscles; at medium range you must leave the ball nestling by the hole, but you are really hoping to hole out; while from point blank range you simply must not miss.

Whatever the range, most golfers do not realise that many of their failures can be put down to poor striking. One who did was Bobby Locke, who, despite the incredible averages that both US and European Tour players achieve per round nowadays, was the best putter I have ever seen. Locke believed that most golfers cut across the ball and so he devised a method that made this well-nigh impossible: he putted with his left foot well in advance of the right and swung the club back quickly inside and almost, it looked, around his right ankle. The Americans, on whose tour he was so successful, claimed that he hooked the ball into the hole and perhaps they had a point, for Bobby Locke certainly always aimed for the right half of the hole. He felt that his method gave him consistency in striking – and that's what you should aim at. Every putt is a straight one, once you have decided the line to hit it along, but you must stroke the middle of the back of the ball with the sweet spot of your putter. If you do not, you may have judged the strength to perfection, but you will always finish short of the hole.

Bobby Locke did not in fact have the perfect putting stroke any more than Lee Trevino or Jack Nicklaus has a perfect golf swing. What all great champions have is a method that they can repeat, so that their worst efforts are not too far away from their best.

So what are the ingredients of an effective putting method?

First, you have to have the right tool for the job. I know of one man who persisted for years using a putter he had bought in a junk shop for a few pence when he started playing the game. He never thought to blame his putter for his fairly woeful efforts. Eventually he began to experiment and then found he was really quite effective with just about any club – except the one he had failed with for so long. As a beginner, experiment. I do not suggest that you buy a whole trunkful of putters, but try out any that you can borrow for a little light exercise on your club's putting green. You may well discover which of the many types suits you best. Remember that the great putters have come up with very different answers to the problem of getting the little white ball into the hole. Johnny Miller and Isao Aoki, for example, almost always used centre shafts. Jack Nicklaus and Gary Player favoured the blade type. Tom Watson and Severiano Ballesteros always used putters with the weight evenly balanced between both the heel and toe. Of course, there are plenty of others for you to choose from. Some that look like branding irons or mallets; other with hickory shafts and/or marble heads; yet another may be a combination of all the ingenuities yet devised by man. Find something that suits you.

Whatever putter you eventually choose, some basic rules must be followed. The most important is that, as you strike the ball, your putter must be moving towards the target and parallel with the ground. You cannot putt consistently well if you jab downwards at the ball, lift up as you strike or do not have the clubhead moving towards the target in a straight line.

I believe the Locke method is best for most of us: hit from inside to out and, above all, avoid cutting across the ball in a right-to-left movement. You needn't carry this to his extreme. Straight back and straight through will also do very well, as long as the clubhead is carrying through towards the hole as you come into contact with the ball. Keep the club low to the ground throughout, for it is far more difficult to get it there as you hit the ball if you have lifted it up as you swing back.

Nevertheless, I would be the first to admit that putting is the most individual part of our game of golf. There have been great putters who have broken this basic rule. Willie Park, for instance, believed that every putt should be sliced. He believed that this helped to hold the ball on line. Billy Casper used a very wristy method; if you putt with your wrists hingeing you must lift the clubhead as you swing away from the ball. Alf Padgham suddenly had the thought that the putt is the golf swing in miniature and therefore started putting with the ball much farther away from him than normal. For a while, around 1936, he carried all before him, so much so that he was considered superior to Henry Cotton and people began comparing him with Harry Vardon.

But these players, for a time, were geniuses on the greens. By the law of averages, you are unlikely to be, so follow the method that is tested by time and keep your clubhead close to the ground and in line with the hole.

BUNKERED!

There are few things more annoying to the long-handicap golfer, or indeed to one with no handicap at all, than to be told that bunker shots are the easiest in golf. To get the ball close to the hole from a greenside bunker is a matter of both touch and artistry. Simply to get it out and on to the green is easy, however.

This is how you do it. For once I am going to allow you to lift the clubhead and on the outside rather than straight back or inside. Set the face of your club at least a little open. Now forget about the ball. Instead, concentrate about two inches behind the ball on that point in the sand where your clubhead will strike. In your mind's eye have the picture of removing a thin layer of sand which, just incidentally, happens to include a golf ball. What you should be thinking of is splashing sand on to the green.

You will need some experience of this basic shot so that you know how firmly to swing. Obviously the distance the sand and ball will go will depend on the speed of your swing.

Recovering from fairway bunkers is a different matter. You can still use your standard two-inches-behind-the-ball shot to

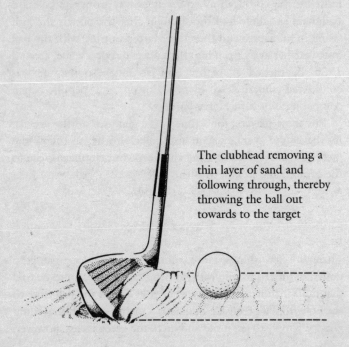

The clubhead removing a thin layer of sand and following through, thereby throwing the ball out towards to the target

get out, but if your ball, sitting cleanly on sand, is not hindered by the bunker face, you may wish to attempt a shot of some distance. In this case it is very much like striking a ball from turf. The problem is that there is almost no room for error. Hit the ball above centre and you will cause it to burrow into the sand. Hit a fraction behind the ball and the power of your swing will be lost. In either case, the likelihood is that you will see the ball still in the bunker and will have to try again.

A little experience should teach you what you can reasonably attempt. Remember, however, that even if you decide you are striking very exactly on a particular day there may be a bunker face in front of you. If it's two feet high and two feet in front of your ball you are going to need quite a lofted club to clear it. Otherwise, there is no objection to using, say, a four-wood or a medium-iron from a bunker if no real height on the ball is needed.

In the Rough

The most difficult club to use from the rough is a long-iron, as I mentioned earlier. From the rough, use the easiest clubs in your bag, the short-irons and lofted woods or a hybrid. If there is a lot of grass between the clubhead and the ball, the wedge or even the sand wedge are likely to be your best answer, and you should also be thinking in terms of the shortest route back to the fairway – even if it's only a very few yards. Otherwise, a lofted wood is likely to be best because it will brush through the grass rather than have to cut its way through as an iron must do.

Hopefully, now you have some idea of the basic skills of the game. Remember, get as much right as you can before you start swinging and it will all become easier and more enjoyable.

5

I WAS THERE

'We've had a great game, Arnold. Let's call it a half.'
The author PETER ALLISS conceding a short putt to Arnold
Palmer on the last green in the 1961 Ryder Cup match at Royal
Lytham and St Anne's

Knowing something of golfing history is a good grounding
for someone coming into the game but it is the great
champions, the great tournaments and matches that really
inspire people to take it up. Most people decide to give it a go
after witnessing, usually on television, some big victory or
astounding deed. Just think of Tiger Woods at the 2008 US
Open. There he was, virtually on one leg, wincing in pain
every time he jarred his knee, but producing some remarkable
golf, some remarkably bad, but also outrageous putts and
amazing chip-ins and eventually holding off the doughty
Rocco Mediate in front of wild galleries. Such memorable
scenes and perhaps more than a few youngsters will even now
be turning to golf rather than some other sport. But the same
applies to newcomers of all ages, perhaps never aspiring to the

level of the top players but just realising what a wonderfully enjoyable game golf can be.

Trying to select some of the great moments from the cavalcade of golf that has unfolded before my eyes since I was a teenager is an enormous task. Where to start? My earliest recollections of great players go back to the late 1940s and early '50s, but trying to convey the excitement, importance and the majesty of victories in those far-off days, when spectators dressed in full-length raincoats, caps and trilbies, is not easy. So I'm going to start with Tony Jacklin's victory at Royal Lytham and St Anne's in 1969.

At that time I was seriously considering retiring from active international play and my work with the BBC was becoming more extensive, so there I was, betwixt and between, working for the BBC alongside Henry Longhurst, hoping for a home victory. Little did we know what a significant year it would be! Eighteen years had passed since Max Faulkner won the Open at Royal Portrush in 1951, the championship having been dominated by Bobby Locke, Peter Thomson, Gary Player. Although a number of great American players had come, not all of them had made return trips to cement their victories. Once was enough for them! Sam Snead and Ben Hogan fall into that category.

Royal Lytham and St Anne's has always been one of my favourite venues, a delightful, unpretentious clubhouse which over the years has become much more sophisticated, but all those years ago it was, to some extent, rather austere. At that time the championship was growing and the R&A were getting bolder and bolder in their course set-ups. Grandstands were introduced, and although in many ways things lagged behind the United States as far as hotel accommodation and the huge amounts of open spaces around their championship courses, it amazed me how resilient and imaginative the powers-that-be were when organising an event of such magnitude. Jacklin was celebrating his twenty-fifth birthday, but all wasn't going so smoothly. The R&A declared that he had an illegal wedge in his bag. Thank goodness he had other clubs with him, so it was just a question of picking one that he hoped would do the job.

The first three days of the championship saw lots of good scoring and many names hovering near the top of the leaderboard. The New Zealander, Bob Charles, had opened up with a 66 but Tony Jacklin was only a couple behind. Bruce Devlin and Peter Thomson from Australia, Christy O'Connor, the amateur, Guy Wolstenholme, Billy Casper and many more were all under par. After 36 holes Bob Charles was still in the lead, his second round a 69, but Christy O'Connor had come in with a beautifully constructed 65, out in 32 and home in 33 on a much more difficult inward nine. Jacklin was still very much in the competition with a second 68. Charles, who had won the championship on the same course in 1963, was a good front-runner, so there was still much to play for. Roberto de Vicenzo came roaring back into contention with a superb round of 66, but one by one they started to falter. Jacklin was scrambling magnificently. Every time he found trouble round the green he seemed to be able to get down in a pitch and a putt whether it be from long grass or sand. In the last few holes of the third round Jacklin started to falter, but time and time again he managed to get down in two. Some say it was the best scrambling they'd ever seen, and Jacklin's 70 gave him a two-shot lead going into the final day. Could he hold on? Hard on his heels were Charles and O'Connor, de Vicenzo and Thomson, while a couple of shots further away were Jack Nicklaus and Brian Huggett. Nicklaus, after a 68 in the third round, was the most threatening of them all.

The final day dawned grey and breezy. Quite a stiff north-westerly wind was blowing. O'Connor had two three-putts in the first 9 and by the 10th he was pretty well out of the competition. On the other hand de Vicenzo was challenging, going out in 33, but after a dropped shot at the 12th he couldn't get fours at the 15th and 17th (both difficult holes into the wind), and dropped away. Nicklaus, like Peter Thomson, played well but the pair of them saw quite a number of birdie putts just failing to drop! The touch of luck they both needed never came. So the championship turned out to be a man-to-man contest between Charles and Jacklin, the Englishman starting with a three-shot lead. It was pretty well cut and thrust until the last four holes where Jacklin still had a three-stroke advantage. But there was still plenty of drama to come – a drive which went off-line, second shots which missed the green and ended up in thick rough. The excitement was intense but Jacklin was still three ahead with a couple of holes to play. He was on the 17th in two but was a long way from the flag and took three putts, whereas Charles got a par-four. Two ahead, one to play. There were at least 10,000–12,000 people gathered round the 18th tee and down the side of the fairway, plus, of course, the anticipation of the spectators in the huge grandstand.

This was the moment of truth. This was the one stroke, the drive off the last tee, that Peter Thomson had mentioned at the beginning of the week and in fact he had written: 'There's a 35-yard patch of fairway about 250 yards down the 18th where, if the opportunity comes, I hope I will have the skill, the nerve and ability to hit one shot straight on to that piece of hallowed turf and go on to win!' The 18th at Lytham was under 400 yards in length but there were two or three bunkers on the left-hand side, a couple down the right, and, near the flag pole, gorse and long marram grass, not the place to go at all! How well I remember Henry Longhurst's commentary as Jacklin unleashed the tee shot. The old boy didn't quite leap to his feet but I remember his immortal words: 'There he goes, oh, what a corker!'

And a corker it was. It scampered down the fairway, across the walkway, leaving him only a short distance to the green. In fact he hit a seven-iron, crisp and true, right into the heart of the green, about twelve or fourteen feet away. Jacklin missed the putt, but that was enough, as Charles couldn't manage a birdie, having driven into the rough on the right-hand side of the fairway. There was much singing and dancing, and why not? Jacklin, the boy from Scunthorpe, had held off a challenge from half a dozen of the best competitors in international golf, and had won his own championship. Lord Derby, who at that time was captain of the Royal Lytham club and also president of Britain's Professional Golfers' Association, presented the claret jug. There was rather a good rendition of 'For He's a Jolly Good Fellow', the odd tear was wiped away and, for the first time in eighteen years, Britain had a new golfing hero.

Jacklin was involved in the tied Ryder Cup at Royal Birkdale later in the summer, with Jack Nicklaus famously conceding Jacklin's putt at the last, a wonderful gesture, although America retained the cup. Then the following year Jacklin went on to win the US Open in wonderful fashion at Hazeltine and he remains the last European to win that championship. Some good years followed but by the late 1970s he seemed to have used up all his ammunition. But he then took up the captaincy of the European Ryder Cup team and steered them to victory, his career resurrected.

The year of 1978 was a remarkable one for a woman of Mexican descent by the name of Nancy Lopez. She won nine professional tournaments, more than any man or woman, and her marriage to a very well known American sports broadcaster, Tim Melton, drew headlines throughout the length and breadth of the USA and, indeed, throughout the world. She had a remarkable five-tournament winning streak in the late spring, and when you consider she was a twenty-one-year-old rookie from New Mexico, who'd had no great amateur career or lived in a world of grand universities and sports scholarships, she was simply phenomenal. Wherever she went she conquered, including the European Open at Sunningdale and tournaments in Malaysia. She won over $200,000 which set a new LPGA record by almost $40,000.

She was inundated with awards, which were not misplaced because over the next few seasons her enormous victory cavalcade continued, and it was through her that women's golf, not only in the United States but pretty well throughout the world where golf was played, received a tremendous shot in the arm.

But Lopez wasn't a one-woman band, there were plenty of other impressive women players around at that time, Joanne Carner, Pat Bradley, Amy Alcott, Sally Little, Sandra Post, Beth Daniel – they all played their part and over the last few years we've had the emergence in women's golf of the wonderful Annika Sorenstam and latterly Lorena Ochoa, another Mexican who has taken women's golf by the scruff of the neck, shaken it, turned it upside down and has done it all with charm and grace. When the Women's British Open was played at St Andrews for the first time in 2007, it was a tremendous occasion. But even though she had faltered in previous major championships, Ochoa proved she was the only one with the game to master the Old Course.

Back to the men. The Millennium US Open Championship was played at the spectacular Pebble Beach Golf Club on the west coast of the United States, just south of the fair city of San Francisco. Tiger Woods arrived with twenty-four summers under his belt and a look of quiet determination. His focus was understandable because this, of all weeks, might be the perfect time and place to win his first US Open. After all, he had won three US Junior titles and three US Amateur titles all in a row, and that would sit nicely with his other two major championships, the Masters which he won in 1997 and the USPGA Championship in 1999.

Very early on Woods created an aura that everybody seemed to notice. Many players were heard to say, 'Well, I know I'm mortal, at least I think I am, but he's certainly not! He's better in every department of the game.' Already the myth started to build up about this young man. Arnold Palmer and Jack Nicklaus were quoted as saying they felt he would win more Masters than both of them put together – and they had ten green jackets! Surely this was an exaggeration? Perhaps not after the way he set off with a round of 65, which was one ahead of Angel Cabrera and two ahead of the American, John Huston. He ended up winning by fifteen shots, the largest margin of victory in any major championship. He also broke the scoring records for fifty-four and seventy-two holes. He was remarkable. New Zealander Michael Campbell, who would go on to win the championship in later years, said he was a freak of nature and worlds apart from all of us in every department. The Woods look, his fitness, the way he hit the ball, the imagination of his short game, the brilliance of his putting – all quite phenomenal. Ernie Els, who finished tied for second place with the Spanish player, Miguel Angel Jimenez, admitted that he would still probably have lost by five or six shots if he'd played above even his great ability.

As each championship went by, Woods drew further and further away, and the powers that be of the United States Golf Association, who are very mindful of their history and do their very best to create a great challenge (at times seeming very sadistic in their course set-up), didn't know which way to turn. Many former committee men had said, 'Well, one thing's for sure, nobody will ever get to 10 under par to win this championship!' But it wasn't to be. Tiger was 12 under for the week of the Millennium Open.

It was also a very emotional time as eight months previously the 1999 US Open champion, Payne Stewart, had died, along with others, in a tragic aeroplane crash, and everyone visiting the 100th US Open was touched by the memory of that flamboyant player. Nowhere did it manifest itself more than at the Tuesday night's Champions' Dinner, the first one, hosted by the USGA. Now this is the practice that has been carried out at the Masters for many years, but for the first time, in their wisdom, the USGA decided they would do it. A hundred US Opens had gone by and they had never honoured their past champions! Tracey, Payne Stewart's widow, was invited to attend the dinner, which she did, and it was a great occasion. The following morning the players and fans bade their fond farewells to Payne with a memorial service along the shoreline of the 18th fairway. It was a very moving occasion and, after a brief service, twenty of the players, all close friends, and Mike Hicks, Payne's long-time caddie, assembled at the edge of the fairway and simultaneously hit balls into the water, providing golf's version of a twenty-one-gun salute. Everything was still and quiet, broken only by the voice of a man, way out in a kayak, who shouted, 'We love you, Payne.' A touching moment and a perfect farewell.

Woods continued to practise and practise. He followed his 65 with a 69 and suddenly was six shots ahead of Thomas Bjorn and Jimenez. One or two slight hiccups in the third round but still a 71, in strong winds, and a total of 205, which put him ten shots ahead of Ernie Els, who had a 68, one of the lowest rounds of the day, but was well back in the field. Woods played a beautifully controlled final round and perhaps might have broken Nicklaus's scoring record of 272 but, when playing the 18th hole, decided to hit an iron off the tee, play up short of the green, pitch up and two-putt for a safe par-five, and the 15-stroke victory. Most, if not all, the field and all the 'establishment' who witnessed those extraordinary four days could not help but think, 'There's no one within touching distance. No one is chipping, pitching, putting, scrambling the way he can and has. If we don't get some competition, if we don't have one or two players stepping up to the plate to challenge, this game is going to get boring.' And all this, remember, happened in tricky, difficult conditions.

For some reason Tiger had set that millennium year as something rather precious. Afterwards he remarked, 'There comes a point when you feel tranquil and calm, at ease with yourself.' These are words I'd heard Peter Thomson utter all those years before and they are facets of human nature that are given to very few. I'm so delighted I've been privileged to see Tiger Woods play so wonderfully well, and the way he works out problems and gets the job done is quite staggering.

How much longer will he go on? Other factors come in – his health, family life, the challenges – who knows? It's impossible to explain the inexplicable. Tiger Woods, a rare and unique talent.

At Turnberry in 1977, we had Tom Watson and Jack Nicklaus going at each other blow for blow, like a couple of heavyweight boxers. The weather was mild, the fairways running, there was little rough and the par of 70 was ripped to pieces, but strangely enough there were only three players who broke the four-round par figure of 280: Tom Watson, the winner, 268, Nicklaus, 269, and Hubert Green, a long way third, on 279. But there was also the lowest single round for an Open Championship at that time, scored by Mark Hayes, and that was 63.

There were lots of good scores but no one really challenged Watson and needless to say Nicklaus, who was desperately anxious to do well as he'd not won since 1972, but had always been in close contention. The big blow came at the 15th hole with Nicklaus safely on the green, Watson several yards off to the left in wispy grass, taking a putter and knocking the ball

Padraig Harrington plays out of the rough in the 2008 Open Championship at Birkdale where he retained the Claret Jug for a second year. A magnificent performance.

My dog Lucy consoles me on a day when I felt much more affection for her than for my putter.

Right They say balance in golf is everything. How about this picture of Geoffrey Paine who played to a handicap of 5.

Below left Fighter pilot and war hero 'Laddie' Lucas, brother-in-law of Sir Douglas Bader, was one of the most stylish amateur golfers of all time.

Below right It was remarkable that Sir Douglas Bader could play golf at all with two artificial legs. Bobby Locke looks on in admiration.

Above Two friends who both loved the game of golf – President 'Ike' Eisenhower and Arnold Palmer.

Above Lee Trevino, playing here at St Andrews in 2000, is pure genius.

Below The great Peter Thomson, a never-to-be-forgotten golfer and a good friend.

Jack Nicklaus and Tom Watson were great rivals but good team-mates in Ryder Cup matches.

Above Seve's unique triumphal celebration at the 1984 Open at St Andrews.

Above Nick Faldo, winner of no fewer than six Majors, must be considered Britain's finest golfer.

Below Muirfield weather is not always kind but the course has hosted some glorious championships.

The Royal & Ancient, St Andrews, is a very special place indeed.

Above A chilly day but splendid for golf.

Below Birkdale again proved a challenging and suitable course for an Open Championship in 2008.

crash, bang, wallop into the hole. Then, at the 17th, Nicklaus, whose second shot was a little heavy, came up short of the green, chipped to five feet and missed. Watson reached the green in two and putted out for a four. So they arrived on the 72nd tee with Watson one ahead for the first time in the game. It looked all over, but wasn't; there was still a lot of drama to unfold. Watson's tee shot found the fairway, whereas Nicklaus blocked his away to the right and was very lucky to stop just short of some dense gorse bushes. Not a particularly good lie but, summoning up all his strength, he managed to smash the ball and with a bit of help from the firm fairway it struggled up to the front third of the green. Watson, on the other hand, hit a majestic iron to within three feet. The crowd went ballistic. But it was not over yet. Nicklaus, after much deliberation, struck the putt and one felt that destiny decreed it would go right in the centre of the hole. His faithful caddie of so many years, Jimmy Dickinson, leapt high in the air as the ball disappeared and, although it looked a forlorn hope that he would miss, Watson still had some work to do. I've looked at the putting stroke to win the championship a few times on TV and he fairly did belt it into the hole, although there was never any suggestion that it was going to spin out.

Watson scored 65 for that round, one less than Nicklaus! They walked off the green, arms round each other's shoulders, with smiling faces, which really told us a lot about them and the spirit of the game of golf.

It was called the Duel in the Sun and at the emotional prize giving it was Hubert Green, who finished a distant third, who came out with the immortal words, 'Well, I don't know about them, but I won the tournament I was involved in!'

I think one of the best rounds of golf Nick Faldo ever played was in 1996 when he won the Masters at Augusta. He was up against Greg Norman who was six shots ahead with a round to go. Faldo closed with a most beautifully constructed

67. I didn't think Greg Norman played as badly as many reporters suggested. Some said there was fear in his eyes on the first tee! I certainly didn't see that. I did see one or two strokes of ill-luck and one or two clumsy strokes. His first drive went a little left, he found himself in an awkward position and a shot was gone before the last day had virtually got under way. A beautiful shot into the 9th green looked as if it might stop three or four feet from the hole but spun back forty yards short of the green. Other shots on the first nine that either were just a little too strong or too weak cost him dearly. A clumsy chip at the 10th compounded by some scruffy putting at the 11th meant he fell farther behind while Faldo was going along quite relentlessly. Faldo appeared to have the beating of Norman pretty well every time they played. Another occasion when that manifested itself was in 1990 when the Open was played at St Andrews. Norman seemed to be the only player who could stop Faldo that year but crumbled in the third round and Faldo claimed his second claret jug the next day.

But it's not only the professionals who have wondrous victories. I think one of the most extraordinary results was in 1981 when Nathaniel Crosby, son of Bing (yes, the great old crooner), got to the final of the US Amateur Championship and beat Brian Lindley at the 37th hole at the Olympic Club in San Francisco. Of all the players who competed in that championship, Crosby's record and playing ability would probably just about have suggested an early exit, but there he was getting through round after round, seemingly always a couple down with four or five holes to play, and wriggling out of the net time and time again. Even in the final he was down and out, but with a couple of holed putts suddenly he was the champion, never to be heard of again!

For me being part of the European Ryder Cup team in 1987 (I was captain of the Professional Golfers' Association), when we won the Ryder Cup for the first time in the United States, was a wonderful occasion. It took place at Muirfield Village, Ohio, the home of Jack Nicklaus, who'd been reinstated as captain of the US team with strict orders to bring the trophy home. The first day was very subdued and Jack was disappointed that the crowd wasn't more enthusiastic in getting behind his team, so he sent runners out to buy lots of little flags. Every home supporter was issued one as they arrived at the club and told to wave it furiously. 'Let's get some atmosphere going, let's send those Limeys home with their tails between their legs.' But it wasn't to be. One after another, game after game went Europe's way, and I'll never forget the rejoicing on the 18th green, particularly from Jose Maria Olazabal, who managed to do a cross between a fandango and flamenco, without damaging one blade of that hallowed grass!

One person I don't think has ever had the acclamation he deserved was Sandy Lyle, who won the Open Championship at Royal St George's on the eastern tip of Kent. The year was 1985. Britain had a lot of good players at that time: Howard Clark, Ken Brown, Paul Way, Nick Faldo, Sam Torrance, Ian Woosnam and Sandy Lyle. The first day dawned with a good stiff breeze blowing, which was helpful on the earlier holes. Lee Trevino, as usual, was full of confidence, but American Peter Jacobsen stole his thunder by going to the turn in 31. Everything was going well until they got to the 14th, known as Suez, where many players came to grief in the championship – sevens and eights were in abundance, Jacobsen ran up a nine, and did tremendously well to finish with a score of 71. The star of the opening round was Christy O'Connor Jnr, who, despite one or two hiccups, had a wonderful run of birdies, ending up with a 64 and was leader at the end of the first day by four strokes! Lyle had a 68 which could have been much better, as he missed a number of putts from six feet or even less. He was driving beautifully; when he was not quite sure what to do with a wood his one-iron served him tremendously well. The weather was dreadful on the second day, with strong winds and rain, waves racing in across the bay; twenty-three players scored 80 or more! But the leaders coped pretty well with conditions, perhaps the most severe since the championship at Carnoustie in 1937. For the first time Jack Nicklaus failed to qualify for the final 36 holes: his rounds of 77 and 75 caused him to miss the cut by three shots. O'Connor could do no better than a 76 and, although he finished up with a couple of 72s, was a few strokes behind the champion at the end of it all.

On the third day Sandy Lyle was paired last with Australian David Graham. Thunder and torrential rain caused play to be stopped for about an hour; however the leaders enjoyed much better weather than the early starters. The scoreboard was interesting – Bernhard Langer and Graham led the way with 209, Lyle, Woosnam, O'Connor and Mark O'Meara were three shots behind, a whole gang of big names were within a handful of strokes. The early starters on that final day came in with some good scores. The Spaniard Jose Rivero scored 68, which put him in good stead. Payne Stewart, who played some of his best golf in a number of major championships, completed a four-round total of 283 and sat back to see whether anybody could overtake him, as the leaders still had quite a few holes to play. It could be argued that Lyle should not, in all truth, have won. Both Langer and Graham fizzled shots away, as did Tom Kite, who was going great guns standing on the 10th tee, and then all sorts of things went wrong and he ended up taking six on one of the few simple holes at Royal St George's. That dented his confidence and he took 34 shots for the remaining eight holes, to be home in 40.

The big turning point came for Sandy Lyle at the dreaded 14th. He drove left in the rough, had to pitch out, was still 200 yards away playing his third. A full two-iron shot (a good one) came to rest just on the right side of the green, some twelve or fourteen yards from the hole. Still it looked okay for a par-five but instead he holed only his second long putt of the week and drew within one shot of Graham and level with O'Connor, and even more significant, one shot better than Stewart, the leader in the clubhouse. Better still was the 15th, a good, stiff par-four of 467 yards – huge drive, six-iron second shot and another good putt holed to go one over par and move jointly into the lead. Lyle must have thought that if he could par the last three holes, which amassed more than a thousand yards, he might be in with a chance, at least of a playoff.

He left himself a testing four-footer at the 16th but down it went. The same thing happened at the 17th – a drive into the light rough, second shot a little short of the green, leaving him a testy shot up the slope, which he scuttled four feet past, but he was up to the task. Just one hole left to go. A lot of people don't like the 18th at Royal St George's, it's been lengthened over the years and the green really was designed to receive a middle iron, not a long iron which is needed to get close today. Lyle hit a big drive and needed a six-iron for his second shot. It looked good but the green slopes away to the left and that's the line his ball took into a grassy little hollow. Not a very good lie, but Lyle attempted to bump the ball into the up slope and let it run towards the hole. Perhaps he wasn't quite brave enough, anyway the ball was always short of pace, hesitated and rolled back to the edge of the green. Sandy fell to his knees beating the ground; he was never a great actor and perhaps he was trying to put on a show of anguish to the gallery but, rather like his wooden-like dance when he holed the putt to win the Masters at Augusta, who cared?

If he could get down in two more, which is not so easy with a big slope and a shot of about ten yards, he had a chance of getting into a playoff. He judged the first putt well, finishing two or three feet past and holed out for a five. Stewart was beaten, but what could David Graham and Bernhard Langer do? There was a lot of toing and froing but both of them needed a par finish over the last three holes to tie with Sandy Lyle. Both of them dropped shots at the short 16th and that really was just about it, although both players got their fours at the 17th, so each needed a birdie at the last to tie. Graham found a bunker with his second shot and took five, Langer went boldly for it only to see his ball go through the green on the right. He had to hole the chip for a playoff and, indeed, shaved the hole before running some five feet past. He had missed and the man who long before had been safely in the clubhouse, Payne Stewart, was the outright second. Sandy Lyle was the first Briton to win the Open Championship since Tony Jacklin in 1969 and was assured of golfing immortality. It wasn't a great championship but a fine result.

The past ten or twelve years have been so dominated by Tiger Woods it's quite difficult to pick out any championship gems he wasn't involved in. There have been a couple of Ryder Cup matches which I found very enjoyable. The Americans on home soil were, for years, impregnable but since 1987 (remember the matches are played every two years) had looked vulnerable. So how would it work out in 2004 when the match was played at the famous Oakland Hills Club in Detroit, with the Americans under the captaincy of Hal Sutton?

The Europeans gave them a real drubbing, winning by 18½ points to 9½, but the match was famous for one or two other points of interest, one being that Captain Sutton had paired Tiger Woods and Phil Mickelson, his two strongest players, together, even though there was supposed to be a feud going on between them. In the end both appeared to play like nervous children who really didn't want to be there, and on occasion didn't appear to care. Together they were awful. So a great victory for the Europeans, and their run of fine play would continue.

The same year also saw an amazing run of form from Vijay

Singh. He won nine times, was second twice and on one occasion came in third, playing in thirty-five events. Tiger Woods on the other hand, playing in twenty-two events, won three, including one world championship early in the season and two rather comparatively insignificant events (when compared to the majors) at the end of the season. It was definitely Vijay's year. He'd been on a remarkable run since reaching the age of forty. Many people hoped the same thing could happen to Colin Montgomerie, but as of today's date that does not appear to be the case.

Todd Hamilton won the Honda, a vast tournament played each year in the fair state of Florida, and our Open Championship in a playoff with Ernie Els at Royal Troon – the second year in a row that an unknown had won our championship; what was going on? But he won it well and played some remarkable shots towards the end of the 72 holes, when his nerves should have been very ragged. He was certainly not overawed in the four-hole playoff with Els, and I for one will never forget the run up he played from the front of the 18th green, using a hybrid club from at least forty or fifty yards, which he managed to navigate to within a couple of feet of the hole. All in all Hamilton was to have a pretty good year, but as he'd been playing for many years, mostly in the Far East, his time at the top was obviously going to be limited. However, he presented a cheerful disposition and made himself very popular with all concerned, which, in its way, gave hope to many journeymen professionals, both men and women.

Neither should we forget Retief Goosen, who had a tremendous 2004, winning on four occasions, including the US Open for the second time, the European Open in Dublin, the US Tour Championship and the Nedbank Golf Challenge in South Africa. Phil Mickelson won the Masters, had been second in the US Open and third in our Open Championship, so it really did look as if things were beginning to even out. For me it was a memorable season and we hoped for more parity between the top half-dozen players sharing the spoils, and more often with the occasional introduction of a new name.

So it looked, as the 2005 season began, that there was going to be some sharing of the spoils. Tiger Woods wasn't going to win everything, dammit. But life isn't like that. There were the occasional shafts of sunlight but, all in all, we are still waiting for eight or ten players to consolidate their game, create more consistency, so they can be regular challengers, as indeed there were in the 1970s and '80s.

We can't leave the marvellous year of 2004 without giving credit to the remarkable Annika Sorenstam, who won ten times during an extraordinary season, and her worst finish was tied for 13th. But she could not defend her title at the Women's British Open, which Karen Stupples, a delightful home-grown player from Deal in Kent, won at Sunningdale by five shots. Stupples had won for the first time in America earlier in the year and the start to her final round will feature long in the memory. Playing as two par-fives that week, the opening two holes present an opportunity to pick up plenty of shots. Stupples did just that with two superb five-iron approach shots, at the first to set up an eagle and at the second it disappeared into the hole for an albatross – five under for two holes!

And coming right up to date, Sergio Garcia's 2008 victory in the Players Championship in Florida was a shot in the arm to us all. For many years, Garcia has been a pure striker of the ball, but over the past season or two his putting has become a bit shaky. That in turn has been talked about a lot, his confidence has dwindled and consequently his scoring has gone up and up. But with his wonderful ball striking, if he had managed to think positively, he could have done much better, even if he had been having between 30 and 32 putts a round.

On the final day at the Players Championship at Sawgrass, the wind was quite strong, the golf course was presenting many problems for the players, Tiger Woods was absent (we'll never know what difference that would have made), but when the tournament was coming to the end it was noticeable that the only name really recognisable in the top few places was Sergio Garcia, which again proves that people of relatively modest skills can perform on golf courses considered by the experts as being too long and difficult.

It interests me to see that more and more members of the press are calling it the 'fifth major'. This title is being promoted by those running the professional side of golf in the United States. But I urge the powers-that-be to say, 'No, we hold that four majors, as with tennis, are enough.' I strongly feel it would be wrong to play down the importance of the majors by increasing their number.

Garcia played magnificently at Carnoustie in 2007 but fell in the playoff to Padraig Harrington. The Spaniard did not seem to know how he lost, having led virtually all the way and having a couple of putts to win that only just stayed out. But what about Harrington? At one point, it looked like he was going to do a Van de Velde – the Frenchman who messed around at the 18th at Carnoustie in 1999 and eventually took a seven to fall into a playoff-finally won by Paul Lawrie. Harrington found the Barry Burn not once but twice but somehow kept his head together to make a six. Then he was very impressive in the playoff, becoming only the second Irishman to lift the claret jug after Fred Daly exactly sixty years earlier. As we go to press, he has just done it again in Birkdale in 2008. Quite remarkable. In the windy conditions, he played with such wonderful control and sealed the victory with some glorious play over the last six holes. Greg Norman, inspired by his marriage to the tennis star Chris Evert, played a splendid part in the proceedings and exhibited all the old skills in the tricky conditions. He could not quite outlast the 'youngster' but for a good old'un to perform so admirably is an example for us all.

6

GETTING TO KNOW
THE GAME

'Nobody ever swung the golf club too slowly.'
BOBBY JONES

If you are a beginner, or even someone who has played for many years, how useful is it to watch the top professionals play? At first glance, not very. They seem to play a game with which the club player is not familiar, as Bobby Jones once said of a young Jack Nicklaus. The power of the modern men's game, the speed with which the club is swished, all in the blink of an eye, is not something any golfer of a certain age should be encouraged to copy. But, of course, you should watch the best in the world at the game you have chosen to play. Watching in person at a championship can act as an inspiration, although with the huge crowds on the course at tournaments you might learn more from watching on the driving range as players go through their practice routines. You can even learn from sitting at home and watching on the telly.

What to look out for? How about the rhythm of a Retief Goosen, the tempo of a Luke Donald, the gentle touch of Ernie Els in a bunker, the short-game wizardry of Sergio Garcia, the smooth putting of Paul Casey, or other more weird and wonderful putting styles like the claw grip of Chris DiMarco, the determination of a Colin Montgomerie in winning all those orders of merit, or never-give-up attitude of Padraig Harrington in winning the Open Championship in 2007 at Carnoustie despite twice going in the water on the last hole of regulation play, and at Birkdale a year later. Not forgetting, of course, the pleasure of watching the genius that is Tiger Woods.

What all players, even at the highest levels, have in common is that at some point they have used a gimmick, or a tip, or a new method and it's worked for a while before eventually the magic wears off. This added ingredient might be a key thought about their swing, a pressure point on one finger, a weight adjustment. Even at the highest level, with coaches and video cameras monitoring every swing and putt, players are generous enough to point out something to another player who has been struggling for a while and, hey presto, it's the tip that transforms their game, and the next thing you know they are giving a winner's speech thanking their fellow player (opponent, really) for putting them right. But I'm aware you might be thinking that what works for the top professionals may not work for you. Sometimes it might, sometimes not. With the tips that follow, I've tried hard to make them adaptable to players of any level of skill. They are just things that I've collected over the years. When your game is off in one department, just have a look through, pick out a couple of suggestions and off you go; you may find the secret.

There are so many different ways of playing golf well. Equally, there are different ways of saying the same thing. So don't blame me if some of the tips don't work, and let me be the first to point out, some contradict each other. However, let's begin with putting.

PUTTING

There have been more tips by far about putting than about any other part of golf. Although there are accepted ways of doing it, there's no accounting for genius. Looking back, Bobby Jones used a very light blade – 'Calamity Jane' he called it – standing with feet very close together. On the other hand his great contemporary, Walter Hagen, stood with feet wide apart. In more recent times, Jack Nicklaus stood hunched over the ball, his right arm acting like a piston; Ben Crenshaw with both arms acting in unison; Bobby Locke swinging the club around his right ankle; Peter Thomson with a very long backswing and almost no follow-through at all; Seve Ballesteros getting lower and lower over the ball with the toe of the club getting higher – not quite to the extent of Isao Aoki but coming close.

Yet the accepted classical styles remain good examples. Amongst these, I would rank the shoulder movement of Bob Charles, the forearm action of Tom Watson, and the wristiness of Billy Casper. Three great putters and three very different ways of doing it. Perhaps, in the end, if you keep your body still and time your swing with a rhythmical back and forward movement, and send the ball at the hole at the right pace, you really ought to be a better putter than most. So here are some general tips that have brought success over the years to not a few. Don't try them all at the same time – the point is to find the ones that work for you.

1 When lining up from whatever distance, pick a spot, say six to nine inches from your clubhead and on line to the

target. Decide your strength and then roll the ball over your selected spot.

2 Keep your putter low to the ground on the backswing. (Yes, I know Peter Thomson picked the club almost straight up in the air!)

3 Keep your head still. Don't look up quickly to see if you've holed it. Hit and listen for the sound of the ball tumbling into the cup, like Harry Bradshaw. Arnold Palmer always thought a still head and body of vital importance and that's why he settled into a locked and knock-kneed stance.

4 Think of your wrists as a hinge on back and forward swing. Your putter head will naturally return square to the ball. In essence, this was Casper's method and also Kel Nagle's, winner of the Open Championship in 1960. This Australian imagined his action as being like the opening and closing of a gate.

5 On the other hand, don't break the wrists at all. Think of the putting stroke as an arm and shoulder movement from the base of the neck.

6 Choose a heavy putter. You won't have to hit the ball as hard. This may prove useful on the slower greens of parkland courses and in the winter.

7 Try a light putter. You may feel free to strike the ball more positively. The lightness may help on fast links greens in particular.

8 Find a putter that suits you and stay loyal to it. When you putt badly, blame your touch or alignment, not the putter.

9 When your putter goes off, try another club.

10 For long putts, concentrate on strength alone and let direction come naturally. Try for a strength that will get your ball into the three-foot range.

11 For short putts, push your bottom hand through at the hole. Aim at a particular spot on the edge, not vaguely at the whole target.

12 Take the putter back with your left arm and strike the ball with your right hand.

13 Think of the putt as a backhand stroke. Your right hand just steadies the club.

14 Always be comfortable.

15 Always have your eyes over the top of the ball, preferably just behind it.

16 Try different stances – closed, square and open.

17 Try different ball positions, from in front of the left toe to near the back foot.

18 Try different grips – all fingers on the club, the Vardon, the reverse overlap and hands spread apart.

19 Vary the distribution of your weight.

20 Point your left foot at the hole or, alternatively, keep it exactly square.

THE FULL SWING

1 Keep your elbows in time with your hips. Tom Watson aroused great interest, during the filming of the BBC Pro-Celebrity series in 1983 at Gleneagles, when he said this was what he always looked for in his own swing.

2 'No one ever swung a golf club too slowly.' This was said by Bobby Jones and featured in his own swing, which had an almost drowsy rhythm. Similarly, the great English amateur Leonard Crawley swung lazily. He didn't seem to accelerate, even in the hitting area. However, it is possible to swing the club *back* too slowly. The whole thing can become too ponderous and rhythm can be lost.

3 Correct alignment of the body along the target line and correct ball placement is half the game of golf. I believe incorrect alignment is easily the most common area of trouble. Good players often find they gradually come to

aim too far to the right and poorer ones set up to the left.

4 Try to feel 'oily' in your swing. This key word may help you to be relaxed and fluent.

5 Freewheel *through* the ball. Don't swing *at* it.

6 Think of the golf swing as a windmill. Your body is the tower and your arms the sails. The great difficulty in golf is to synchronise the body turn with the arm swing.

7 Good leg action is the foundation of the golf swing. Leg action is essential for rhythm and balance and helps keep the club going along the target line. I am amongst those who think, however, that leg action is not by any means as important a source of power as some have argued. Seve Ballesteros could hit the ball 250 yards, either seated on a shooting stick or on his knees, while Bob Toski managed 230 yards on one leg. The great Jack Nicklaus became an 'arms and hands' man, whereas he used to believe much of his power came from his legs.

8 Good golf is played with the hands and arms. Bad golf is played with the body. Don't hit at the ball with your navel or heave with your shoulders.

9 Feel yourself hitting past your chin while your head remains behind the ball.

10 Feel your feet rocking on the backswing, not lifting. Have your weight on the pad underneath the big toe and rock to the inside of your left foot.

11 Swing against a firm left side and throw the clubhead towards the target.

12 Nothing should resist your follow-through. Slide your knees towards the target. Perhaps Byron Nelson was the first great player with this philosophy, while Henry Cotton was the most important advocate of the firm-left-side theory.

13 If you get blisters and sore places on your hands, your grip on the club must be faulty, allowing movement. Practise without a left-hand glove to check. Indeed, don't slavishly

wear a left-hand glove. Most players, however, apparently find that wearing a glove is helpful and it serves as a reminder that golf is a left-sided game. Max Faulkner, 1951 Open champion, used to argue that if using a glove on the left hand gave a more secure grip, then surely wearing one on the right hand would be equally beneficial!

14 Keep the club as low to the ground as long as is comfortable on the backswing. It helps to stop you lifting the club up and stretches the muscles.

15 Make sure your left shoulder swings back at least so far that your back is square to the target.

16 Don't break your wrists early. This will help you make a good shoulder turn.

17 Break your wrists early. This helps set the angle of the backswing and you can then go on with the body wind-up. When I won the Italian, Spanish and Portuguese titles in a row in 1958 the one thing I thought about, after I'd taken aim, was breaking the right wrist as I moved the clubhead away from the ball. I then kept it in that position and drove through the ball to a good finish. It was terrific. I couldn't miss. I was disappointed when the season came to an end and I had to wait until March for action to begin again. Alas, I then found I'd lost most of the magic. Not a problem the professionals have today with an almost fifty-week schedule.

CHIPPING

1 Set your weight towards the left side and have your hands well ahead of the ball at both address and impact. This is illustrated by both Gary Player, who produced a chip that ran and checked (rather than floated and checked), and Lee Trevino, who allowed very little follow-through.

2 Imagine you are bowling the ball towards the flag with your right hand. The clubhead should feel an extension of that hand as you float your palm towards the hole.

3 Feel you are striking the ball with the back of your left hand. This helps to keep your hands ahead of the club-head, vital in good chipping, and is Lee Trevino's method.

4 Pick the spot where you want your ball to land, just on the green, and select your club accordingly.

5 Concentrate on becoming confident with just two or three clubs. Some players use only the one and vary the kind of shots they play with it, opening and closing the face and varying the height by the angle of their swing into the ball.

6 Chip with a club that will give little backspin, the six- and seven-irons especially. The more lofted clubs can confound even a good shot when the ball checks unexpectedly.

7 Get used to every club in the bag for chipping. It's perhaps a rather old-fashioned concept, but Henry Cotton once said he used his one-iron more from around thirty yards than for full shots.

8 Keep your wrists out of your chipping stroke. This is likely to suit those who putt with a shoulder movement.

9 For short chips, try using your usual putting grip. Many top players use their reverse overlap grip and it's at least worth a try. But don't be greedy and use it from farther and farther away from the green.

THE SHORT PITCH

1 Make your sand iron or your lob wedge your friend and practise with it. As these clubs have the most loft they will give you the most backspin and you may have the feeling

of placing the ball very near where you want it to finish. You'll have to move the ball back in your stance, however, so that the leading edge of the club is nearer the ground than the rear flange.

2 Or the reverse. Play with the ball positioned well forward in your stance and the blade of your club open. Have both feet turned slightly towards the hole with about 70 per cent of your weight on the front foot. Hands must be kept ahead of the clubhead.

3 Imagine you are playing off a pane of glass or marble. Better still, actually do so. If you can flick the ball off the surface you'll be well on the way to excellence.

BUNKER SHOTS

1 Think in terms of throwing the sand underneath your ball, as well as the ball itself, on to the green.

2 To vary the length of the shot, hit into the sand nearer and nearer to the ball, thus increasing your distance. Start about three inches away.

3 Always play from sand with a firm grip and keep the clubhead moving through the sand.

4 Switch to your wedge or nine-iron when the sand is hard and wet. Your sand iron may well bounce.

5 Make sure you have a sand iron that suits both you and the bunkers of your home course. In general, for soft seaside sand a heavy club with a deep flange or low rear edge is best. A thinner flange may be better on clayey inland courses, as the shot becomes more of a pitch. If you find the right club, keep it when you part-exchange your irons for a new matched set.

6 Slide the clubhead under the ball from right to left and keep the clubhead moving towards a full follow-through.

7 When the ball is buried in soft sand, consider realistically what the alternatives are. You may well be better off playing out sideways. There are two ways of playing the shot when all is not impossible. One is the Chi Chi Rodriguez method, as I call it. Open the blade of your club, keep your hands well forward, break your wrists and drive the clubhead into the sand behind the ball, and keep it going deeper and deeper in the general direction of Australia. The shock waves will remove your ball, with some height. The other method, which will work if the bunker's face is not too high, is to close the club face and strike the sand between one and two inches behind the ball; keep the clubhead moving to a full follow-through.

8 Most bunker shots fail because the player doesn't hit firmly enough. Practise a little and you'll find that you can hit full out and the ball won't go very far if your club enters the sand well before the ball. A snatchy, twitchy stroke is death to good bunker play.

Well, there's my brief selection of tips. When you come across one that works for you, be sure to make a note of it. Many of the great players have learned that the memory can play us tricks. Even if the magic fails totally in the years ahead, if you've written it down, it might well come in useful for as long as you play the game.

One of the wonderful things about golf is that it has such an effective handicapping system. This means a poor player can still compete against a good player, provided each plays to his or her handicap. There are other ways in which the game can be adapted to allow differing standards to be accommodated, whether it is the various formats or the different teeing grounds. Typically, a hole will have a series of tee markers making each hole play longer or shorter. Perhaps rather unfortunately, these have traditionally been referred to as for seniors, women, men and finally men's medal tees, which are the back tees reserved for club competitions. In addition, there may be championship tees, further back still – these days way, way back – which are used by the top professionals playing in a tournament. Really, these different tee markers simply allow anyone, regardless of gender or age, to play the course at a yardage that suits their game. Choosing a set of tees suitable to your game can add significantly to your enjoyment of a round of golf; playing a course that is simply too long can become something of a drag and unnecessarily ruin the day.

It may take beginners a while for their game to settle down and become consistent. He or she may find, if lucky, that the ability to hit the ball a fair distance comes quickly but that touch on the short game takes very much longer. I found that I could hit the ball vast distances easily, without forcing every ounce into the shot. I was also a fairly good putter. Yet it took me many years to develop what skills I had at those little high-floating shots or low runners from seventy yards and closer to the flags. So it may take a while to develop a realistic handicap, which can be earned by playing in club competitions and submitting properly marked scorecards to the club secretary. Once you have a handicap, that tells you how many strokes you should play the course in above the Standard Scratch Score, which is determined by the par of the course, its length and relative degree of difficulty. So if the SSS is 71 and you have a handicap of 23 and score a 94, then you have played exactly to your handicap.

Clearly, the better you get, the lower your handicap becomes. A handicap of zero is known as 'scratch' and a 'plus handicap' indicates a top amateur player who ought to play the course in less strokes than its SSS.

A handicap not only allows you to monitor how you are playing, it also allows you to play against other people. There are many formats to allow for this. Medal, or strokeplay, is the form used most often on the professional tours and for the great championships. No need for handicaps at that level, but for the club monthly medal, your handicap is subtracted from your gross score to give a net total. Matchplay is the original format of the game and can be used by both singles and pairs. Each hole is a mini-match in itself, with the player with the lower score winning the hole. If the same number of strokes are taken by each player then the hole is halved. The scoring is determined by how many holes 'up' one player is. The outcome is decided when one player or pair is more holes up than there are left to play. So a match in which a player goes five-up on the 14th green results in a 5 and 4 victory. When players have different handicaps, the difference between the numbers is the number of shots awarded to the higher handicapper. These shots are designated at holes as determined by the stroke index of the course, which is the listing from one to eighteen as to the difficulty of each hole. So if a nine handicapper is playing a sixteen handicapper, then seven shots are awarded at holes with strokes indexes one to seven.

In a variation on this format known as bogey, a player plays a matchplay game against the par of each hole. So a net birdie or better is a hole won by the player, a net bogey or worse is lost. In a group, the player who is finishes up by most holes is the winner.

One of the most traditional forms of the game is foursomes. In this format there are two players on each team and they alternate shots with the same ball. By agreement, one partner tees off on the odd-numbered holes and the other on the even-numbered holes. A variation is greensomes whereby each partner tees off on each hole and then they pick the ball in the best position and alternate shots from that point. Alternatively, in fourball better ball, each partner plays the hole with their own ball and the lower of the two scores becomes the team score.

A completely different format was developed by Dr Frank Stableford, whose name it is known by. This is a points system: one point is scored for a net bogey, two for a par, three for a birdie, four for an eagle and five in the rare instance of an albatross (or double eagle as it is known in America) and represents a score three less than the par of the hole. One great advantage is that if a player cannot get his bogey, and therefore score a point, he picks up his ball rather than continuing to play and rack up a high number as the medal format requires. This helps the speed of play and however disappointing a 'blob' might be, it is less humiliating than putting a nine or a ten on the card as he would need to do in a medal round.

One of the drawbacks of golf, particularly if you are playing in a fourball, is the time it takes to play. This was something that concerned Peter McEvoy, one of the finest British amateur players, as he saw new, shorter formats like Twenty20 cricket take off. Was there a golfing equivalent, he wondered? His solution was to come up with Powerplay golf, which is played over nine holes or any loop of say seven, eight or ten holes. The difference is that each green has two holes cut on it. One is in an easy position, the other in a far more difficult location. Before teeing off, the player nominates whether to go for the easy or the hard flag. The reward, if playing a Stableford, for example, is that if you go for the harder flag then the points for a birdie are doubled to four and for an eagle to six. The aim is for each player to make more decisions about risk and reward, thinking more about their course management. So while it might be a shorter and quicker version of the game, it is also more intense. Ideal for a summer's evening or a winter's afternoon. Whether it will take off on a grand scale we have to wait and see, because it is against the inclinations of the dyed-in-the-wool traditionalists, but it could be a saviour for people starting out, or for those with only a short time to spend out on the golf course.

What other sport allows players of vastly differing standard to compete with each other in such a simple way? Whatever the format, whatever your handicap, or whatever tee markers you use, there is one truism in golf: if you can play your own game – against the course, not the opponent – you will survive and even prosper.

Let's turn to the actual business of hitting the ball. Although it is the methodical touch players who usually come out best, I would by no means decry the sheer animalistic thrill of smashing full out into the ball with a driver. I remember the days of my youth at Ferndown when I used to pick up every old ball I could find on the course and save them until the end of the round. Then I would go to the edge of the putting green and try to drive across what were then the eighth and ninth fairways and on up into the woods that bordered Lone Pine Caravan Camp. Ah, the bliss of it all when everything in the swing was exactly right at full power!

Perhaps few of you, especially if you come late to the game, will experience the joy of sending a ball on a journey of 300 yards. Yet the appeal is little different when, within your capabilities, you launch into the ball and everything goes far better than normal. Perhaps this will be a drive of 220 yards – but the feeling is much the same if 190 yards is the distance you're used to.

What does the average keen golfer so delight in about the game that he will go out every day of the week, come rain, shine, high winds or chilled hands?

Golf is as highly competitive as any other game and there is little to equal the thrill of a first win in a club competition, perhaps with a trophy to stand on the mantelpiece for the rest of your life or until the next club annual dinner. Yet many golfers ignore club competitions almost entirely. Perhaps they play in a sufficient number to retain their handicap – or never bother to have an official handicap at all. But there will still be competition. It may be the chap you play with every Sunday morning or a regular fourball. In either case there is the pleasure of winning – and, of course, the frustration of losing a match which was nearly in your grasp. Above all, the game is there to be enjoyed. Don't ever allow yourself to wander the course in a cloud of gloom.

Although I've begun by emphasising long driving as a basic delight, that is just a small part of golf. One of the strongest features of my own game, for instance, has always been long-iron play. Many would say that the feel of a perfectly struck two- or three-iron loses nothing in comparison with the perfect drive. It's a test of accuracy as well; how near that distant flag has the ball come to rest? Long-iron play is the part of golf where the greatest weaknesses show themselves. A modern innovation reflects this with the new crop of hybrid clubs (Rescue Clubs), which offer the flight of a long-iron with the easier striking of a fairway wood.

As you move to the short-irons you are into the precision game. It is no longer a matter of how far you can hit the ball, but whether you have chosen the right club and hit the ball the right distance along the target line. There is perhaps a different kind of delight in deciding just what sort of shot you want to play and then judging and executing that shot to perfection.

Ah yes, putting, the game within a game, at times the great equaliser of both small fry and the great names alike. As the old-time Open champion Willie Park used to declare, 'The man who can putt is a match for anyone.' Obviously, any idiot ought to be able to get the ball into the hole from, say, eight feet. Yet all too often we have to shrug our shoulders as the ball pulls up short or tantalisingly curls around the rim. From two to four feet it is even more infuriating when the ball obstinately remains above the ground.

This distance was my greatest weakness as a tournament golfer. As a youngster I had no difficulty in rattling them in without pause for thought, but then a world-famous professional told me that I would never be much of a putter with the grip I was using. I heeded the great man's words – and never felt comfortable again. However, I was never quite as bad as my reputation and my car number plate – PUT 3 – imply. I must have holed plenty to win some twenty tournaments and five national championships, but there were more than a few others that slipped away as the short putts slid past the hole.

If you can play the long shots steadily, pitch reliably and putt consistently, you will, off your handicap, be a match for anyone.

7

QUESTIONS AND
ANSWERS

*'Golf instruction books can be immensely valuable to the
novice. What you do is balance one on top of your head
and then swing the club as hard as you can. Once you
have mastered the art of taking a full vicious swing
without dislodging the book, you can play golf.'*
PETER DOBEREINER, *Dobereiner on Golf*, 1996

I can't remember when it happened but it certainly surprised
me the first time a fresh-faced youngster approached me with
a proper autograph book, a smiling face, and asked me for my
autograph, saying how much he'd enjoyed listening to me on
television and following the game, sitting in a comfortable
chair at home, but had I actually ever played golf myself. I
think it took me quite a few seconds to recover from that
blow. The question was asked at least twenty-five years ago
and I, perhaps conceitedly, believed that anyone who had
followed golf at all knew the Alliss family connection with the

game; after all it's not an everyday surname and might have stuck in someone's mind! It taught me a lesson, I can tell you!

Over the years the questions have come in thick and fast. Let's take a few general ones to start.

'Who's the best golfer you've ever seen?'

That is an impossible question to answer. You can't liken then and now. There was a period sixty years ago when the name of Ben Hogan stood out head and shoulders above anybody else, then along came Arnold Palmer, Jack Nicklaus, Gary Player, Lee Trevino, Ray Floyd, Peter Thomson, Tony Jacklin, Nick Faldo, Johnny Miller, Greg Norman, Bobby Locke – a whole host of wonderful golfers. And then, in the early 1990s the name of Tiger Woods appeared. He had just won his third US Amateur Championship and was on the threshold of turning professional, and he immediately roared away from the rest of the golfing world.

At this moment there is not the shadow of a doubt that Tiger Woods is the finest player on the planet and, although he gets lots of accolades, in a strange way I compare him to Byron Nelson, who dominated golf at the end of the Second World War. Nelson won eleven tournaments in a row and eighteen for the year of 1945 – an amazing achievement, but the criticism was that the 'big boys' had not returned from the war and he had no opposition. In my opinion that didn't matter a jot, just look at his scores – he was averaging just over 68 for the competitive rounds played, quite remarkable. Tiger Woods has beaten that particular record and now dominates every event he plays in.

Is he a giant amongst pygmies? I think there's a very good case to answer there. Battles between David and Goliath, Gulliver and the Lilliputians are not for this period of our history. He's coming to his absolute prime just when the good contenders are going off the boil – Ernie Els, Retief Goosen, Darren Clarke, Colin Montgomerie and a host of others, like Jim Furyk, who for quite a long time held the second best player in the world position only to hand that over to Phil Mickelson.

And what about those early golfers? Bobby Jones, the greatest amateur of all time, dominated the world of golf from the mid-1920s to the early '30s. And what about those players from the late nineteenth/early twentieth centuries – Vardon, Taylor, Braid? From 1900 on they put together a series of amazing scores using clubs that looked antique even when they were new, golf balls that were hardly round and golf courses looked after mainly by cattle and sheep! Athletes from the 1930s, '40s and '50s have produced records which perhaps are scorned today but they were the best of their time and that's all we can judge them by. Let's just marvel at the skill of Tiger Woods and think how fortunate he might be not to have Watson, Trevino, Nicklaus, Palmer, Player, Floyd, Faldo, Ballesteros, Norman, David Graham and Larry Nelson snapping at his heels.

Next question: How has modern equipment changed the game?

Looking back to the early days of golf, it's quite amazing how well the players performed with the implements of the day. There have been several milestones in the game's history, the coming of the rubber-cored golf ball and the introduction of steel-shafted clubs, so although there were changes from the early beginnings, it wasn't until the late twenties/early thirties that major changes started taking place. Since 1950 dozens of golf equipment manufacturers have attempted to beat the system, by that I mean produce clubs and balls that conform to the rules and regulations laid down by the Royal and Ancient Golf Club of St Andrews and the United States

Golf Association, but would give the players using their equipment a slight edge and encourage a very gullible public to invest in their wares.

It's not easy to select any particular item that stands out more than any other, but I do believe the most important advancements as far as quality and consistency goes is in the golf ball. The name of Titleist springs immediately to mind, a company that for decades has produced golf balls of the highest quality. They joined up with the shoe company Foot Joy to create a wonderful business empire. Taylor-Made, Ping, MacGregor, Mizuno, Wilson and, although outgunned by the aforementioned, Dunlop and Slazenger still have a share of the market. The number of manufacturers has dwindled over the years; golf equipment now is very highly specialised and millions of pounds, dollars, and yen are spent on trying to perfect new and revolutionary golf clubs that will do practically all the work for you, with titanium shafts, metal heads made from all sorts of wonderful materials, grips, all offering something special. Technology has changed all sports, but those playing have also contributed to many changes.

Golf courses are kept in far better condition than they were fifty or sixty years ago, and fifty years before that the introduction of the cylindrical mower for cutting fairways, tees and greens was a wonder and revelation for the green-keeping staff of the day. Bunkers are now carefully looked after, and rakes, drinking fountains, halfway houses, toilets, practice grounds all provided. Things will continue to change over the coming years, but I still think those golfers of a hundred years ago were, in many ways, cleverer, more talented, had more imagination than a great number of today's so-called golfing stars. In other words, if used correctly, for someone with even a modicum of skill, new equipment has made the game easier.

Next question: I'm asked if, in my opinion, the game is run well at the highest level.

The answer to that is simply yes. Although it's not perfect, the majority of the rules and regulations which control this wonderful old game are made by amateurs with a love of golf. Nobody can create anything for their own advantage, certainly not for monetary gain. Apart from the two great bodies in Scotland and the United States, there are many other legislative committees operating in every country in the world where golf is played, all basically adhering to the conditions laid down by the USGA and the R&A. The world of politics is going through a very unhappy period with accusations of greed and lining pockets. Perhaps the world would be a better place if amateurs with no axes to grind were running things, looking with a clear and honest eye, attempting to sort things out in the fairest possible way. Pipe dream? I guess so.

Next question: Women and men in professional golf, how do they compare?

At the highest level of competitive golf there are three categories, Women, Men and Seniors (now playing what is known in America as the Champions Tour). The main men's professional tour in the United States keeps going at a most extraordinary rate. Most people, including myself, have wondered how long it might be before the bubble bursts. Every week there's a first prize approaching one million dollars, and although the mighty dollar has taken a beating over the last year or so, it's still an awful lot of money for knocking a golf ball round 130 acres of well-manicured turf and sand! The other two, women and seniors, have fluctuated rather over the last twenty-five years. There was a period when senior men were making serious inroads into the livelihood of the women. Lots of big names hit fifty and plied their trade in another age bracket – Palmer, Nicklaus, Floyd, Trevino,

Watson, Irwin, Player, the list goes on and on. The Champions Tour took off like a rocket, one of the reasons being people in executive positions who were investing in a golf tournament to advertise their businesses were of that sort of age. They'd been brought up with those famous names and were quick to jump on that particular bandwagon. But steadily new faces began to appear on the Women's Tour, players from Scandinavia and Asia were making their mark, and a young bonny lass from Mexico by the name of Nancy Lopez really did attract spectators through the gate.

The prize money for the seniors and the women tournaments does not compare with the main Men's Tour but it's still a wonderful way to make a living if you have desire, skill and good nerves. Television companies have tried to blend the three together. This was brought about by Terry Jastrow, who for some years was Sports Producer at ABC Television and a very forward-thinking man, who introduced the Wendy's Challenge (Wendy's being one of the big hamburger fast-food chains in the United States). He took someone from each tour and brought them together in a competitive sense, each playing from a different tee, leaving the same sort of shot into the green for everyone. Then there was the Three Tour Challenge, a similar operation, and one of a number of programmes made specially for TV which are played out as a run-up to Christmas. Years ago the people in charge of the PGA Tour were very mindful of the power of television and didn't like their stars to go off earning money that way instead of playing in tournaments they were fighting hard to organise, but a balance has been found and as far as I know there's not much complaining going on.

Of course, with such great inducements now for players with skill, the days of having an amateur career have gone. The only people turning pro now over the age of twenty-five are those good amateurs who decided to give the Seniors Tour a go the moment they hit fifty. So if you have a child who shows promise, you should think about introducing him or her to the world of professional golf. If you make the grade, it's very lucrative, but you need more than a couple of attributes. 'What are they?' you say. Obviously a healthy body, a steady, cool, calculating brain with a portion set aside for all things golf – balance, rhythm, talent, nerve, desire – and something no one can legislate for, your share of good luck!

Next question: Private jets and all that. 'How many players have got their own private jets, Peter?'

That's a question I never thought I'd be asked when I retired from international play after the 1969 season.

Of golfers I think Arnold Palmer was the first to learn to fly a plane – that's forty years ago. Not sure whether he bought one outright, had it on HP, or the business of leasing had come into operation. Jack Nicklaus followed, so did Chi Chi Rodriguez and a number of lesser pros who went in for more modest machines, which had such things as propellers, turbo-assisted, but they did have inside lavatorial arrangements! I remember well playing in the 1967 Ryder Cup at the Champions Club near Houston, Texas, when Arnold Palmer arrived and zoomed over the course in his newly acquired plane, which was a small jet; I could hardly believe it! A number of years ago some bright spark introduced the idea of leasing by the hour, which has become very popular indeed. Buying a plane outright is a huge capital investment, running into millions of dollars. How are you going to use it? Are you going to get value for money? Arnold Palmer, I was informed, used to lease his out, thereby covering much of the plane's cost. Jack Nicklaus, on the other hand, allegedly had two pilots permanently on standby and used his jet to fly hither and thither to see his boys performing in various football matches up and down the country.

But, for me, if I had their money, the greatest thing would be to have a decent-sized pumped-up helicopter – I think they're wonderful machines. I've even got the pilot picked out, an ex-officer in the Scots Greys by the name of Francis Davey. Now for me that would be a luxury.

Next question: What is your favourite type of golf course and why?

Very easy. I was brought up at the Ferndown Golf Club, a few miles north of Bournemouth, with its heather, pine, gorse, silver birch. Every club in the area of Bournemouth and Poole has those characteristics. I suppose it's the Scots pines, gorse and heather that really captured my imagination, for, on a winter's day with a blue sky and the sun shining, even though it may be below freezing outside, the view from the window of the clubhouse overlooking the putting green, down across the first fairway always delight me. The gaunt majesty of oak and elm, is grand in its way, but give me heather and pine every time.

Next question: Why are there so few tournaments played in the British Isles these days?

It's interesting to look back and see how the pattern of tournament golf has changed over the years. The season used to begin with the Sunningdale Foursomes, an excellent competition which is still played to this day round the Old and New courses. Any combination can partner each other in foursomes – amateurs, pros, women, men, all coming together towards the end of March when hopefully the weather is beginning to be kind. Moor Park, near Watford, was usually the scene of the first professional tournament of the year and there were various events culminating in the Gleneagles Foursomes played in the second or third week of October. Interspersed with that there were a number of continental championships, which were always a delight to play in.

As the world of professional golf grew bigger and bigger, it was necessary for the powers-that-be to spread their wings, thereby producing more tournaments for European players to compete in, and that could only be done by following the sun. It was very soon realised that golf, particularly in Britain, was only viable from the beginning of May to the end of October, and even then you needed a modicum of good fortune to see you through.

The American circuit was growing and growing but they could only accommodate 150 players at any one time and over the years a second, and even a third, division of tournaments were set up, with a promotion and relegation system which gave more aspiring professionals a chance to show their skills. For some reason professional golf in South Africa, and indeed the rest of Africa, hasn't taken off as it did in New Zealand, Australia and Asia. Japan, however, went through a period of having a thriving home circuit which operated at a very high level of competence. But that didn't fill the needs of all the hungry players anxious to make a name for themselves.

With that in mind, the European Tour administrators, led at that time by Ken Schofield, decided to branch out to see whether the various tours would co-sanction events in their areas with the European Tour. Now this was stretching geography to its limits. They began the new season before the old one had finished. How can that be? Well, tournaments were played in November, December, leading into the events scheduled for early January, thereby creating a year which ran for the best part of fifty-eight weeks! It means a tremendous amount of travelling, not only for the players but also the administrators, caddies and everyone else connected with professional golf.

For many years there have been tournaments played in Australia, New Zealand, parts of the African continent, South Africa, Central and South America, but they were never quite big or bold enough to make any real impact on the world of golf. As soon as those countries discovered a really tip-top player, male or female, they left to try to make their mark in golf either in Britain and Europe or the United States. Over the last few years the pattern has changed and, although it is a long way to travel to Australia and New Zealand, many more young players from around the world are finding their way to the wonderful golf courses down under. The prize money has improved, and with the advent of the boom in golf in China and, more recently, India, things are really on the move.

For many years there has been a thriving tour for both men and women professionals in Japan; many great players over the years have emerged here, but they didn't travel. There was no need, they were so successful at home. Tournaments in Central and South America are few and far between, with not a huge amount of prize money, but they are growing. I'm sure that when those countries see how golf is taking off in Asia, they may well attempt to join the bandwagon. Also new golfing countries are opening up in Europe.

Prize money on offer now is staggering, I marvel at its continuing success but sometimes wonder whether the bubble will let out a little air, or indeed burst, in my lifetime. I hope not, but those in high places must be aware that there has to be a limit on prize money provided by great companies, particularly when the world is going through economic change and disturbance.

Now for some specific questions I've been asked over the years.

Professionals always take off their gloves when putting. Amateurs seldom do. Why is this?

The golf glove plays a very important role, particularly in relatively modern golf. They were first introduced in the 1930s and the most prominent player of the day, from the European point of view, was Henry Cotton, who used them to good effect. The thinking was that a left-hand glove (for a right-handed player) gave a better grip on the club. The reason why a lot of professionals remove them whilst putting, and indeed in some cases for shots within twenty to thirty yards of the green, is because they get a better feel of the club, thereby allowing them a more delicate touch. A number of good amateurs use this method, but it's not on the whole necessary for the club golfer.

Next question: If you see one of your opponents improving his lie, thinking you haven't noticed, is it better to say nothing?

They say you can call a person anything but a cheat at golf. Should you see anyone improving his lie you can handle it in several ways, either by putting on a grim face and accusing him vehemently, or treating it in a jokey way, thereby shaming the miscreant by the fact you've noticed what they're doing. In some cases players are oblivious to the fact they may be cheating. For example tapping the ground behind the ball when it's in light rough is illegal, but it is done often enough. It's all in the way you handle it, but *do it*, don't let them get away with it.

> 'You know the old rule. He who have fastest cart never have to play bad lie.'
> MICKEY MANTLE, *Esquire*, 1971

Next question: Is it true that a threeball has no standing on the course and should let a fourball behind them through as soon as they hold them up, even for an instant?

In club golf there was until recently no place for a threeball, therefore it had no real standing on the course. It came in the same category as someone playing by themselves. If they're playing so slowly and the fourball or foursome coming up behind is moving along faster, then they should let them through, but sadly the courtesy of calling people on when you're either looking for a ball or just playing slower seems to have disappeared. Even in the professional ranks it never happens, and that is one of the reasons why play is so slow. It can, however, be rather confusing, since many, indeed most, professional tournaments throughout the world are always played in threeballs.

Next question: If the players in the game in front of you are desperately slow, is it rude if you ask them to let you through?

It is certainly not rude to ask them, but do so with a smile on your face, e.g. 'Gentlemen/ladies, you seem to be having a few trials and tribulations. Would you mind if we go through? We're playing quite fast and I'm sure it would help/improve/make your game more enjoyable and it certainly would for us.' Then get out of the way as quickly as possible.

'It is a law of nature that everybody plays a hole badly when going through.'
BERNARD DARWIN, *Playing the Like*, 1934

Next question: Club professionals seem to encourage members to buy a complete set of clubs from one manu-facturer. However on TV one often hears that tournament pros have a mixed set. Why is that?

Club professionals have a mixed set of clubs because the important clubs are the two or three most lofted clubs, putter, driver and, shall we say, 'rescue' (better known as a four- or five-wood years ago). They may well hold on to these treasured clubs, while changing the others. Putting is a very individual thing and many golfers have a putter made by the same company which produces their full set of irons, but there are so many models of putter with different weights, lies, length, it's so much a personal choice. I'm sure there are golfers in your club who have a favourite club of some sort or other which they are very loath to part with.

Next question: I was never very good at tennis or cricket, or other moving ball games. Does this mean I probably won't find golf any easier?

Golf differs from all other games, apart from snooker, because the ball is stationary. Hand and eye co-ordination is an important factor, the game is much more pedestrian than others but it's a question of rhythm and balance. For those of you starting out I do urge you to book half a dozen lessons, have them in close proximity to each other and at the end of that time you'll know whether you have any aptitude for the game and whether you are going to enjoy it.

Next question: I notice at the golf range that 90 per cent of the golfers are practising off the rubber tees with their woods and long-irons. Is that more sensible than practising chipping and putting off the mat? Surely the short game is just as important as the long game?

Golf ranges have played a very important part in the growth of the game, but because you are playing off rubber or fibre matting, a rubber tee has to be used. Remember, driving ranges are one of the first stages in the operation of learning to play, so hitting off a tee makes getting the ball away easier and gives you a feel for the shot. When you are a little bit proficient you can attempt to play short-irons straight off the mat, thereby building up confidence in hand and eye co-ordination. Use a low tee for long-irons and build up confidence.

Next question: I never feel confident that I have lined up my putter accurately for putts over three feet. Is there an obvious method of checking? I heard you mention spine angle on TV – is that something I should know about?

Putting is a game within a game. Very few people practise diligently and there are reasons for that – it can be very boring and it makes your back ache! But, if you have access to a decent putting green, get four or five balls, place them in a circle round a hole no more than eighteen inches away and knock them in one at a time. Take your time, line them up, be comfortable, tap them in. You're getting used to seeing the ball go into the hole. Then move six inches farther away and so on until you get to about the four-foot mark. You'll miss some, but take your time, again building up your confidence, and have a little competition with yourself to see how many you can hole. Also invest a few pounds in a putting lesson from the pro; he may sell you a new putter but that, in turn, may be well worthwhile. Trust him, he will give you good advice. As far as spine angle goes, that's just one of the many modern clichés which have crept into the tuitional side of golf. It used to be, 'When driving, imagine you are seated on a shooting stick.' Heigh-ho, nothing much changes!

Next question: Is it true that in Spain and Portugal you have to wear plastic-studded golf shoes and not the metal-studded golf shoes that some players still use?

Many of the courses on the continent have gone over to plastic studs in golf shoes. The idea was that metal studs were more likely to tear the grass, causing snags. It's not compulsory at the top echelons of golf to use plastic spikes, and I would say the majority of players still use metal studs, because they give you a firmer grip. At least, that's what the players who use them believe, and confidence plays such a huge role in the game of golf.

Next question: I tend to hook my pitching wedge and short-irons, hit my seven- and eight-irons surprisingly straight, but I slice my long-irons. Please help me.

The shorter the club, the greater the loft, the easier it is to get the ball away. The most difficult clubs are those with the longer shafts and less loft, i.e. driver, two- or three-iron. Why? You are standing farther from the ball, the swing arc is wider, there are more things to go wrong. That's why, over the last few years, the shorter 'rescue' clubs have come into their own. Some of them are only the length of a six-iron, with a lot of loft and a big head. They can and indeed have revolutionised the lives of club golfers. Again, seek out your pro and let him straighten out that slice.

Next question: I am going to France later this year. Will I simply be able to play on arrival at a golf club, or should I phone first? My French is bad. Will I have to prove I have a handicap at an English club?

When travelling abroad it's always wise to take a handicap certificate with you, or some form of identification that lets the powers-that-be know you are a bona fide golfer. If you are playing at one of the lesser-known golf courses you should have no trouble in getting a game, but it is wise to phone first, or, if you are staying in a hotel, get the concierge or someone to ring on your behalf and enquire about the rules and regulations appertaining to visitors.

Next question: When one plays a chip shot should the hand be locked at impact?

The great thing about chipping is the hands should always be ahead (in front of the clubhead). Line yourself up, 'break' your wrist, then leave your wrist there, leading through with the back of the left hand, hitting down and through with rhythm. Don't flick at the ball, let the loft on the club do its work.

Next question: My opponent temporarily lost his ball in the rough. On finding it just under five minutes later, he played the ball safely on to the fairway, meanwhile losing his Havana cigar in the same rough. I rejected his request to have a further five minutes looking for the cigar. Did I act correctly?

I think if your golfing compadre can afford to smoke Havana cigars he needs cultivating! As long as he doesn't set the whole course on fire I would search desperately to find his cigar before the Fire Brigade do! Who knows, he may offer you one; if not, a share of his Mars bar.

Most unusual question: I have just started to hook my shanks. What should I do?

Keep it to yourself. Never mention it again. You're on the slippery slope to oblivion. I suggest you look for another pastime. But then, on the other hand, you may be one of the rare breed of shankers who not only perpetrates that dastardly deed but are 'carriers'!

8

HOW TO ENJOY YOUR GAME

*'I enjoy watching first-class golf; but I have long ceased
to study the methods of first-class male golfers. After
the age of 50, it is more profitable to watch the best
women golfers.'*
LORD BILL DEEDES, *The Grown Ups Annual*, 1990

Bob Hope once said, 'If you find golf relaxing, you're not
playing it properly!' There may be more than a few
curmudgeons out there who get some sort of perverted
pleasure out of embracing the frustrations that the game can
throw up, but if golf is to be the cure for the Grumpy Old
Man then it should be enjoyed. And that means more than just
enjoying the surroundings, the fresh air and the company.
With a little thought and a little effort, you can enjoy your
game, too!

The first thing to realise is that the advancing years will have
an effect on your golf and it is only sensible to compensate

accordingly. Golfers come in all shapes, sizes and many categories, but as one gets older I think those who have played golf at a high level are perhaps the ones who suffer the most.

It is some years now since Gary Player and others of his vintage were regaling one and all with the information that, due to modern technology, they were hitting the ball as far as they did twenty to twenty-five years before. Sadly, as the years went by, that glorious situation faded. There aren't many golfers today at the age of sixty-five plus who can hit the ball as far as they did years ago, even with the help of today's magical equipment. So, if it happens at that level, how about those less talented? This is where we need to take stock of the situation.

Some years ago I found myself in the company of Lee Trevino. We were going off to play a few holes. Now Trevino is a few years younger than I am but, as we approached the first tee, I noticed he strode past the back tee and made his way to what could only be termed 'the members' everyday tee', not a million miles behind the ladies'. I made some flippant remark about going from the 'girls' tees', to which he replied, 'You and I have both spent enough time battling from back there,' pointing to the 'tiger' tee, 'now it's time we played where we can get the most enjoyment!'

Think about that for a moment. Lee Trevino, in my opinion one of the greatest players of modern times, was suggesting that he had no desire to play from the back tee, hitting two-woods to every par-four, he wanted to play for the sheer enjoyment of the game, and of course he was right.

This attitude can percolate down to you, no matter what your handicap. It may mean you will no longer compete in the monthly medals. So what? Put your ego away and move forward, so golf becomes pleasurable instead of a series of monstrous slogs on the long holes. Why worry if your handicap has gone up from 9 to 11 or 11 to 16? Providing you are just as canny as you were in the old days, people will still complain you're a bandit! The handicap system is there to give people of varying levels of skill a chance to play against each other in a competitive way. It doesn't take long to find the real imposters, those masquerading off a false handicap – they get their own sadistic pleasure out of that. Let them be.

Rather like trying to lose weight, everyone is looking for a magic pill, a cure, a thought that will do it for them without any real effort on their part. Sadly, that's as unrealistic when it comes to playing better golf as it is for losing the pounds. A plan is required but where to start? As we have seen, as you get older you will lose some power and will need a driver with more loft. Years ago, if you told people you were driving with a 'spoon', three-wood, call it what you will, they thought, 'Hey, you'd get much more distance with a "proper" driver.' Not so, my friends, the longest drivers in the world today, and by that I mean the professional big hitters who compete in special long-driving contests and not in normal tournaments, invariably use clubs with more than 10 degrees of loft, some of them even going up to 12½ degrees, the idea being to launch the ball quickly, up and away, so that it gets maximum carry. If you have such a club, with a little bit of practice you can use it off the fairway and then you only need a four- or five-wood, a rescue club, utility or whatever, to fill that department of your game.

Now for the irons – I doubt whether you need anything lower than a four, so a four, five, six, seven, eight, nine, pitching wedge, sand iron and putter make a full set or, if you are looking to lighten your carry bag, you might settle for just the odd numbers – three, five, seven, nine, pitching wedge and then something with about 56 degrees of loft that will get you out of bunkers and, with practice, will serve you well round the greens.

Don't forget golf balls are made with many different degrees of velocity. There's one that will suit your particular game better than another. Take time to find out, ask at the professional's shop.

Treasure your equipment. If you use a glove, look after it, they are expensive; having an old glove with holes, all shiny, does you no good at all. The same with your grips – they need looking after, give them a wipe, a wash, clean them at least twice a year, you'll feel the difference immediately. But once they've gone too far, rather like the tyres on your car, have new ones fitted. Yes, it's an expense, but you're playing golf for your enjoyment, so make the most of it. It will only take a little effort but the rewards can be enormous.

Having sorted out your equipment, the next thing to consider is your state of mind when you get to the golf course. Why, you might ask? Well, golf truly is a mirror of life. Some players arrive at the golf club in a great hurry, always behind schedule, even on their big day – playing in the final of the captain's prize, or whatever. They screech into the car park, rush into the clubhouse, no time for a chat, grab some golf balls and tees, get on to the first tee just in time, opponent waiting, no chance for a practice swing or even a putt or three. The result? You knew what was coming – usually a scuttle along the ground or one out of bounds and the chances of getting a good one away pretty well eliminated from the moment they got up in the morning. The other type of player gets there a little earlier, takes out his pipe (when smoking was popular and enjoyable), sits for a moment on the edge of the putting green watching the old dog fox go by at the end of the 17th, listens to the early birdsong, hits a couple of putts just to get the feel of the greens, then makes a few swings and half a dozen hits in the net just to break down the 'adhesions'. All in all a gentle soul, ready to take on the young buck, who's a bit of a Flash Harry. Off they go, down the middle, the older, mature man just short of the green in two, chip up, two-putts – five net four, and so the story would go on until the shake of the hands on the 16th green, a victory for the quiet man 3 and 2, and platitudes spoken through gritted teeth, 'Well done, best of luck in the next round.'

What all players should do before beginning to play is to have a few 'practice swings' beside the first tee before it's their time to tee off. I've put the phrase 'practice swings' in quotes because in my opinion they are nothing of the sort. Two vital ingredients are missing: a golf ball and the feeling of striking it with the clubface. Every club should have a practice net adjacent to the first tee. Not many club golfers seem to have the strength of will to go off to the practice ground (if there is one!) and a net is at least a partial answer. Alas, this facility is all too rare or very badly maintained. The mat may be worn out, the netting hangs limp and is often in holes so that it's positively dangerous. If practice nets are available, many golfers will make use of them and they are invaluable for warming up. They get you swinging and, more important, give you the feel of striking a ball. Good players have enough feel in their hands to know what kind of shot they have hit.

If you can make the effort to arrive half an hour early, head to the practice ground with just a dozen balls, twenty at most. This is just a warm-up, not a full practice programme. Don't reach for the driver. First, I want you to get into the golf swing gently and loosen up the joints and muscles with a simple exercise or two which take no more than a couple of minutes.

1 Slip a golf club behind your back and hold it there with the insides of your elbows. Now turn from left to right (gently, gently, gently!) just as you do in a normal golf swing. Make sure you make a really full shoulder turn and get your back facing the imaginary target. Be gentle and work up until you feel you are stretching your muscles and sinews.

Starting to get the muscles moving

2 Now start swinging the arms as well, keeping the full
  shoulder turn. Avoid doing this violently. Be gentle, trying
  to feel yourself rhythmically into the swing.

Keeping the arms swinging gently . . .

3 My next exercise aims at helping you get the feel of the clubhead. Take the club in your hand and swing it back to about hip height and gently through the hitting area. Concentrate on rhythm and knowing where the clubhead is throughout.

4 Now put it all together, particularly keeping the shoulders turning and feeling where the clubhead is throughout your swing. Don't begin to thrash at your imaginary ball. Aim at a full backswing and gradual acceleration down.

... Now add the club

You are now ready to use those dozen or so balls. Hit most of them with the pitching clubs, then hit a couple of mid-irons and finally tee one up and give it a crack with a driver or three-wood. Then, if your club has a practice bunker and you are a fairly poor sand player, it will do you no harm to pay a brief visit to show yourself that you can still get out.

Lastly, two or three minutes on the practice green. You should have two main aims. The first is to give yourself confidence in holing the very short ones. Start at little more than a foot away – you can hardly miss from there! The sight of a few putts disappearing into the hole will give you confidence if you have to hole a two- or three-footer for a half on the first green. Finally, have a few long putts. There is no need to aim at a hole. Just try to get the feel of your fingers coasting the blade into the back of the ball along the chosen line. Aim at striking your ball in the sweet spot.

You are now ready for the first tee.

After these very simple procedures there is no reason why you should not go out and play the game of your life. You have just gone through most of the things that will be required of you on the course. You will be looser than your opponent and feeling more confident than most of your fellow players if they have arrived a minute or two before teeing off. You may still not win, but you will have avoided starting with an in-built disadvantage.

Warming up is an important part of playing better golf but there is much you can do even before you head out for that vital match in the club knock-out. I can't stress enough the need for practice. That doesn't necessarily mean hours out on 'misery hill' hitting hundreds and hundreds of balls willy-nilly. You're far better off having a maximum of twenty balls, which you might keep in one of those plastic tubes that were very fashionable years ago, or just a dozen or so balls in a bag, easy to carry and it affords you an opportunity of concentrating on each and every shot. That was the advice my father, Percy, gave me years ago: 'It's better to practise with a dozen golf balls and try your very best to play the correct shot, every time taking perhaps twenty-five or thirty seconds over every shot, than having a bag of fifty balls and hitting them one after the other, machine-gun fashion without a thought in your head!' How right he was!

There might be a time – happy days! – when you are in top form and hitting balls on the practice range is just a matter of keeping the feel and the rhythm going. But there will inevitably be faults that need attention – not even the best players in the world are perfect in every department of the game. Many club golfers, if they go to the driving range, end up doing what they do well. For example, if they are a good driver, they like to watch the ball fly up and away. I can hardly blame them, as it's a lot more fun than patiently working on a weakness, but if you can make an improvement to an area of your game that is not as strong as others, then you will lift the whole level of your game. If there is one certainty in golf, time and again it will put you in the situations in which you are least comfortable. And whatever type of shot it is, if you step up to it feeling that a disaster lies ahead, disaster will result, flukes apart.

It is on the practice ground, not the golf course, where you can experiment and build up some confidence. Let's suppose your wedge play is giving you cause for concern. Faced with a shot of, let's say, eighty yards to the flag, you have no idea how far the ball will fly. Sometimes it climbs skywards and falls well short, at others it bores quite low through the air and you finish through the green. You realise that is no good at all. Consistent length with the wedge is vital. A problem like this is almost certainly caused by your hands sometimes being in front of the clubhead at impact, while at other times they are behind. You may find that hitting a dozen or so shots free from the pressure of being on the course gives you the feel of the club and, suddenly, the problem disappears. If not, changing the ball position in your stance may do the trick. The key is to experiment until you get a reasonably consistent height of shot.

At the other end of the spectrum, you may want to practise with the driver, given that this is one of the most difficult clubs to use for the simple reason that the shaft is the longest and the clubhead has the least loft of any club, putter excepted. The greater length of the shaft makes it more difficult to control the clubhead, and the straighter face increases any tendency you may have to hook or slice. But ask yourself a question: should you be practising with the driver at all? Perhaps not before you've become a fair to good player with a three-wood. Almost every beginner and even moderately good club golfers will get a better *average* length with this club and will hit far more fairways.

Whatever type of shot you are practising, think about what you're trying to achieve and aim at a target. After each shot, stop to consider it. If it was good, why was it good? Don't hurry to try to repeat the performance but instead fix the feeling of that successful shot in your memory. Often you will find it was rhythm and balance that did the trick. Hardly ever will a full-out flail at the ball deserve the credit. A few specialist shots require some special comments:

IN THE BUNKER

Most high handicappers are frightened of the bunker shot because they remember previous failures from sand. Confidence is totally lacking; fear predominates. Yet if you head to the practice bunker for any length of time, you will rapidly lose most if not all of your fear. The sand shot is possibly the simplest in golf and the sand iron is the easiest club to use, designed with a single purpose in mind – to get you out of that bunker.

Of course, I don't mean you'll turn into Gary Player or Ernie Els in the twinkling of an eye. What I can promise you, however, is that you will soon learn to play the uncomplicated bunker shot with confidence. You will soon learn there is really not all that much to it. Just hit a couple of inches or so behind the ball and keep the clubhead going. In a trice both your ball and the sand beneath it will be on the imaginary green. In no time, you will learn to get the ball out with very fair consistency. Getting out of a bunker does not require a great golf swing; what you need is the ability to strike accurately at a particular spot in the sand. And confidence. Once you have that essential confidence, you are well placed to get distance and precision from greenside bunkers.

PITCHING

Pitching from fifty to eighty yards is one of the weakest shots of most club golfers. It really ought to be possible to knock the ball in the air and land it somewhere near the flag. Yet how few can do this consistently. It most certainly is an area of your game where you can hope to improve enormously with practice. In the average fourball, the golfer who can play this shot well prospers and will collect most of the side stakes. The only problem is that on the practice range, the ball will not react on landing as it does on a closely mown, well-prepared green. But what you need to aim for is that your batch of balls should all end up in as tight an area as possible, with no wild strays.

CHIPPING

Chipping does not need a splendid swing. Mainly, you need the ability, which should come with experience, to judge the run of the ball in the prevailing conditions. And you also need confidence. You must feel sure that you can strike the ball as you intend so that you can concentrate on the pace of your miniature swing rather than worry whether you are about to top the ball or scuff the ground in front of it. The aim is to send the ball on to the closely mown surface of the green and then let it run towards the hole. I would advocate learning to play most chip shots with one club, which many of the modern-day professionals do. Or you can use a variety of clubs, starting with that little chip and run from a yard or two off the green where a four-iron might be used. If you are a good long putter and a rather poor chipper, you could do worse, especially when the ground is either frozen or soft, than use the putter from, say, ten yards off the green. You may be able to judge the run of the ball better.

PUTTING

Long putting is a matter of touch, judgment of distance and striking the ball in the sweet spot. Short putting, except for the occasional little curly ones, demands that you should be able to knock the ball a short distance dead straight, with rhythm and tempo. For both lengths, you need good nerves and confidence, and I'm afraid I have no magic words or pills for either. Your own confidence will have to be the answer and, to a greater or lesser degree, that will come from practice, from knowing that you can do it because you've done it many times before.

On the short ones – and who isn't a little unsteady over those three- and four-footers? – start from somewhere around the one-foot mark and bang them in. You can then introduce a drill that might be boring but is extremely effective. Insist to yourself that you must hole every ball from one foot. Then you go on to, say, six balls from a foot and a half. Gradually get further away, but if you miss one, then it's all the way back to the beginning. At college Colin Montgomerie used to do something similar before dinner. He would have to hole a hundred – yes, a hundred – consecutive two-footers before he could go and eat. The first ninety or so weren't the problem but when it got down the last few, with the Scot's tummy rumbling, then the pressure was on.

When practising your longer putting, don't worry too much about the line. It's the pace that is important. You are aiming for a three-foot circle around the hole and if you don't get in it, you have either misjudged the length or actually mishit. Judgment will come with practice and experience, while a proper strike is a matter of finding the sweet spot on the putter face. Once you have improved those skills, it might be worth getting a friend to check your alignment so you know you are actually aiming where you think you are!

Getting more specialist help with your game is the next step. After all, although I have preached the need to practise, it is no good practising your faults. This is where your local professional will be invaluable, for a couple of lessons where he can show you the various routines of shots around the green, the difference between a pitch shot and a chip shot, the sort of clubs you might play for a variety of shots. There are some common faults and an expert eye will be able to tell you soon enough if they apply to you:

Your backswing is as fast as your downswing.
You're lifting the club up, not swinging it.
Your knees are as stiff as a guardsman at attention.
You're hardly turning your shoulders at all.

You're starting back to the ball before you've completed your backswing.

It's all far too hurried and snatchy.

You're not using your right hand at impact. It's dead.

Your right hand is overpowering your left.

You're turning your shoulders away from the target as soon as you begin the downswing.

Your head and body are lifting up to follow the ball before you've even hit it.

You're trying to scoop the ball up into the air. Let the club do it for you and hit down and through the ball.

Making changes to your swing can take some time but it is worth it. You'll probably become frustrated but if you get yourself on the right track and have the right information fed into your own mental computer, it won't be long before you see how it works. You'll begin to get the feel of it and that builds confidence, and you'll be on your way. Remember, get as many things right as you can *before* you actually draw the club back – I can't stress how important that is. If your alignment is wrong, if your grip is ill-conceived, if your weight distribution isn't good, the chances of you correcting during the swing are very remote. Of course there are limitations. If you are a late starter it is even more important to get the right sort of grounding.

The ideal time to start stick and ball games is when you're young, *you get hand and eye co-ordination*, but that doesn't mean to say that if you start when you are over forty years of age you can't become proficient. And always remember your handicap – it's there to help you. If you learn to use your strokes wisely you can make yourself into a formidable opponent or excellent partner. If you get the opportunity to watch golf at the highest level you'll notice it's not always the brilliant shots which bring success, it's the few silly, wayward, stupid, careless or reckless shots that have caused the problems. Eliminate those, or a percentage of them, and you will see a great improvement.

Much of what I've said applies equally to women golfers. It is more difficult for woman to give the ball a whack because the majority aren't as strong as men, and don't have strong arms and wrists. It seems that few women are able to use their wrists in the 'proper way'. Imagine yourself practising a left-handed backhand shot at table tennis – you take your hand back, looking down to see the watch face, you bring it to a straight position and then turn it away so you see the under-part of the strap of the watch. That, in a simple way, is the way to whack a golf ball. At the top of the back swing you can more or less turn your head to right or left (depending on whether you are right- or left-handed) and see what time it is. Most women find it difficult to get their hands in the right position at the top of the backswing, so it is much harder to hit the ball sharply.

However, balance and timing are so important, and in this area of golf the majority of men could learn a lot more from watching women professionals than looking at Tiger Woods and his contemporaries. Make the most of your talents, punch your weight, sweep the ball away. When you're driving, set the ball high, even if you have to hover the club slightly above the ground before you take it back. Try to sweep the ball off without knocking the tee out of the ground; this will show you are swinging the clubhead back into the ball at the right angle. Don't hit at the ball, swing through it.

I realise how my own game has changed over the course of the decades. When I was a teenager, I delighted in smashing the ball as far as I could with the driver. I had much the same aim with all the clubs. I liked, for example, to crack a full eight-iron straight at the flag and delighted in seeing the ball kick, bite and spin back. Not for me the gentler pleasures of pushing in a six-iron for much the same result, perhaps shaping a low one, with just a bit of fade, working out where to pitch it so that my ball would follow the run of the ground to the flag. I still had much to learn. Not for the young Alliss much thought of playing a fade to the right half of a fairway if there was out-of-bounds on the left, perhaps with a three-wood. This is the sort of thing that Henry Cotton meant when he said of a young whippersnapper: 'Oh yes, you say he hits the ball well. That's all well and good, but can he *play*?' It is all very well hitting the ball well, as I always felt I did, but playing the right shot at the right time is the key. A mixture of splendid shots and foolish errors never leads to good scoring.

Learning a consistent fade from the tee was perhaps the most important part of my development as a player. I certainly believe it is more reliable than drawing the ball. A draw runs and runs, all well and good if it is down the middle of the fairway but not if it runs into bunkers or rough. The faded ball stays pretty much where you put it.

The other important step in my learning process concerned the short game. I was much less competent at floating a pitch on to the green from fifty yards than at other aspects of the game. Fortunately Ken Bousfield, who at the time had the best all-round short game in British golf, took me under his wing. What he emphasised was that a long backswing was essential. 'Give yourself room,' he would say, 'and then float your blade into the ball.' I learned to give myself room and to vary distance by learning to feel the pace of the clubhead into the ball. This is the opposite of what you can see on your own golf course any day of the week: a short takeaway that hardly reaches knee height. With so little room to work in, the player has almost to shove the clubhead at the ball with his hands. He has no feeling in the shot at all.

After I had stopped playing competitive golf I certainly enjoyed the game more, and worried about it less. But I never stopped learning. Above all, I learned that golf is different – but no less enjoyable – for those whose sheer physical strength has grown less as the years have passed. It's just that there is less power and the challenge is to adapt your game.

Take a shot from a tight fairway lie with around 200 yards to go to the green. Once I would have reached for my two-iron. Now I take a four-wood and try to hit a high fade landing to the left of the flag and then rolling towards the hole. All the time, I try to think about what kind of shot is needed. Should it be moving from right to left, or from left to right? Should it be high or low, or a runner or full at the flag? What is the condition of the ground?

I have also learned that, with getting much less practice, slight mishits are far more likely. And over-clubbing is far better than using the club that will just get you there, provided you keep an easy rhythm and control the pace of the clubhead through the ball. Yes, I could get there with a cracking eight-iron but there is no real trouble behind the green and so I'll hit a six-iron, firm but not full out, and have the feeling of floating it to the target. As for playing out of the rough, well, my wrists are about an inch less in circumference than when I was in tournament practice. So I cannot force the ball out of bad lies as I used to. Instead, I take the short route back to the fairway with a lofted iron.

It is all a question of knowing your own game and capabilities. You'll enjoy yourself more and score lower. No one can be as good as they were in their prime but you can certainly enjoy the game as much, if not more.

9

HOW TO HELP OTHERS ENJOY THEIR GAME

'Caterpillars were turning into butterflies in the time it took him to play some of his shots and he even tossed up bits of grass to check the wind before he disappeared into the trees for a call of nature.'

Sports writer MARTIN JOHNSON commenting on the slow play of Belgian professional Nic Vanhootegem at the 2001 European Tour qualifying school, *Daily Telegraph*

Unless you are playing quietly by yourself, perhaps just after dawn or in the long summer twilight, which can of itself be a pleasant way to enjoy the game, you will inevitably be playing alongside other golfers. Golf has changed in many ways over the years, especially at the club level, and we'll get to that later. But change is unavoidable in the modern world, and it is some of these changes, perhaps sometimes necessary, often seemingly unnecessary, that infuriate the Grumpy Old Man. Another thing that often gets up the nose of the GOM is rules for rules' sake and within club golf this might often be the case – watch out or you will be told what you can wear, when, and in which room of the clubhouse, that sort of thing! But the Rules of Golf themselves are very necessary, certainly when you think of all the different conditions, the different terrain, the different circumstances in which golf can be played all round the globe. And then there is the etiquette of the game – something that sounds a bit old-fashioned these days. Really it is about being sensible and respectful – of the golf course on which you are playing and the people with whom you are playing. It is all about making sure everyone can enjoy their game. As in life, it's someone who decides they're the only one who matters and they'll do it their way that is guaranteed to make everyone else exceedingly grumpy.

Perhaps the biggest curse on the game today is slow play. The game is getting slower and when that happens it gets boring for players, viewers and commentators. It happens at all levels but it is at the professional end of the game where it is most obvious. Actually, on television, they do a good job of covering it up by switching to a player when he is about to hit. But even then, the overrunning becomes obvious when the scheduled finishing time is long gone and other programmes have to be shifted out of the way. That might be acceptable on a dedicated sports channel but it makes it very difficult for channels who have other things to show. Amazingly, the last twosome in the final round of the 2008 Masters, including the winner Trevor Immelman, took over five hours to play their 18 holes. Five hours! Pity the spectators along the fairways who have to stand and watch while nothing continues to occur before finally someone takes a shot.

And, of course, so many people copy what they see the professionals doing on television – endless practice swings, elaborate methods of alignment, glove on, glove off, marking the ball on the green after every putt, cleaning it and replacing it just so. These rituals become so engrained they can't even tap in a putt from two inches without going through a whole routine which takes thirty or forty seconds. Everyone talks about slow play but nobody does anything about it, and nothing will happen until the players themselves decide to change, until they say, 'Hey, come on, we can save a minute, perhaps even two minutes a hole. If each of us does that, we've knocked half an hour off our round, and nobody damaged, nobody upset, nobody rushing round the course like a whirling dervish.'

It is not about sprinting around the golf course. It is about being ready to play. What does it mean to be ready to play? Well, if you have a strokesaver, for example, consult it while you are walking up to your ball, not once you have got there. Equally, have an idea of what shot you want to play so that you only need to reassess after checking the lie. If your fourball is in a chatty mood, don't just go from one ball to the next continuing the conversation, each player should be already at his or her ball ready to play. In foursomes, where alternate shots are taken, the partner who is not hitting can be walking on towards the next landing spot. Don't stand on ceremony. Yes, there is an order of play, with the farthest away playing first, or maybe someone who is off the green coming on before everyone putts, but there is no penalty for playing out of turn unless it is a proper matchplay competition, when a player could have a shot replayed. Otherwise, just get on with it, as long as everyone else is aware of what you are doing. Watch each player's shot. This is not only respectful, and might save injury if a shot skews off in an unexpected direction, but can speed things up if a ball ends up in the rough or the trees and a search needs to be undertaken. If such a search holds up the group behind, then let them through. Leave your bag or trolley on the side of the green closest to the next tee (there is often a sign) so you can clear the green quickly. And if you're competing in a medal competition or a game that requires a card to be filled in, do so when you get to the next tee. Don't hover round the green holding up the game coming up behind you, get on to the next tee and fill your card in while your opponent/partner plays his tee shot. That all helps to knock seconds/minutes off a round, so, without doing anything radical, the game can be played at a more refreshing pace.

What else to bear in mind? Replacing divots on the fairways, repairing pitch marks on the greens (not spike marks) – not just yours but others', the surfaces of the greens recover more quickly than if they are allowed to remain – don't 'throw' the flag down on the green, don't stand too near the hole, tearing the grass with your spikes, whether they be soft or metal, don't tread on the line of someone else's putt. I believe that bunker rakes, a relatively recent introduction, should be left in the sand, not outside, because in that position they can cause a ricochet, for either good or bad. If there is no rake, just smooth the sand out with your feet rather than try and do it with a club.

What about bad temper? A poor shot can cause people to get extraordinarily cross but while the occasional thrown club or swear word might be tolerated among friends, it can all too quickly become a habit, and not a very appealing one to fellow golfers you are playing with for the first time. No one gets angrier than Tiger Woods on a golf course but once he has walked ten yards down the fairway, he leaves it behind and plays the next shot as if nothing had happened. What a mind he has!

Golf is a game of trust. A golfer walks alone. There is an onus on the golfer to be honest as he plays a round and cheating is not only frowned upon, it is just not tolerated. The man (or woman) who cheats is always the loser. But the Rules are there to help you and a working knowledge of them can make the game faster and more enjoyable. The R&A, who are the guardians of the Rules in this country and most of the world, produce a small booklet and it is useful to carry it in your bag – then you can check on something if it comes up in a round. But beware, no one likes a pedant who whips out the Rules at every suspicious moment – and it is likely to hold up play!

There are some basic rules that it is worth knowing and it is also worthwhile reading the opening section of the R&A booklet which offers some basic advice, remarks on etiquette and gives the formal definitions as used in the Rules. Knowing the definitions is extremely useful when it comes to deciphering later rules. So here are some pointers to get you going:

THE TEEING GROUND

The teeing ground is the starting point for the hole to be played. It is a rectangular area two club-lengths in depth, the front and sides of which are defined by the outside limits of the two tee markers. If your ball falls off the tee peg, or is knocked off as you address it, it may be re-teed without penalty. If a stroke is being made in these circumstances, that stroke will count, but there is no further penalty.

HAZARDS

A hazard is any bunker or water hazard. The key thing to remember is that you cannot ground your club in a hazard. A bunker is a hazard consisting of a prepared piece of ground, often a hollow, from which turf or soil has been removed and replaced with sand. A water hazard is any sea, lake, pond, river, ditch, surface drainage ditch or open water course (whether containing water or not) and anything of a similar nature. All ground or water within the margin of a water hazard is part of the water hazard. The margin of a water hazard extends vertically upwards and downwards. Stakes and lines defining the margins of water hazards are in the hazards. Water hazards (other than lateral water hazards) should be defined by yellow stakes or lines. A lateral water hazard is a water hazard or that part of a water hazard so situated that it is not possible or is deemed by the committee to be impracticable to drop a ball behind it in accordance with Rule 26–1b. A lateral water hazard should be defined by red stakes or lines.

When a ball is lost in a water hazard, the golfer has two options, under penalty of one stroke in each case. He can drop a ball as nearly as possible at the spot from which the original ball was last played, or drop a ball behind the water hazard, keeping the point at which the original ball crossed the margin of the hazard directly between the hole and the spot on which the ball is dropped. There is no limit as to how far behind the water hazard the ball may be dropped.

When a ball is lost in a lateral water hazard, the golfer has these two options, plus one other to consider. Another ball may be dropped not more than two club-lengths of (1) the point at which the original ball crossed the margin of the hazard or (2) at a point on the opposite side of the hazard equidistant from the hole. The ball must be dropped and come to rest not nearer the hole where the original ball last crossed the margin of the hazard.

LIFTING AND DROPPING THE BALL

The original position of the ball should be marked (for example with a tee) before it is lifted. If this is not done, there is a penalty of one stroke and the ball should be replaced. If the ball or marker are accidentally moved in the process of lifting or marking, there is no penalty. The ball or ball-marker should be replaced. A ball being dropped under the Rules should be dropped by the player standing erect, holding the ball at arm's length and shoulder height and dropping it. If it touches the player, his partner, either of their caddies or their equipment before or after it touches part of the course, it must be re-dropped, without penalty. A dropped ball shall be re-dropped without penalty if it: rolls into a hazard; rolls out of a hazard; rolls onto the putting green; rolls out of bounds; rolls to a position where there is interference by the condition from which relief was taken; comes to rest more than two club-lengths from where it first struck part of the course; rolls and comes to rest nearer the hole than its original position. You must drop the ball at the nearest point of relief, even if some other obstruction is then in the way – you then take relief from that point.

'If he takes the option of dropping behind the point where the ball rests, keeping in line with the pin, his nearest drop is Honolulu.'
JIMMY DEMARET on Arnold Palmer on the rocks at the
17th hole at Pebble Beach, 1964

PROVISIONAL BALL

The business of playing a provisional ball often causes great uncertainty. In plain terms, if you think your ball may be lost or out of bounds, to save time you can play a provisional ball from the spot where you played the original ball. You must tell your partner or opponent that this is a provisional ball. If you don't, the original ball is considered lost and the provisional ball becomes the ball in play, under penalty of stroke and distance. You can keep playing a provisional ball where it remains short of where the original ball was lost. If you play the provisional ball from the place where the original ball was lost, or from a point nearer to the hole, then the provisional ball automatically becomes the ball in play under penalty of stroke and distance. If the original ball is not lost, the provisional ball is abandoned, any strokes with it are ignored, and play continues with the original ball.

Loose Impediments

Loose impediments are natural objects such as stones, leaves, twigs, branches and the like, dung, worms and insects and casts or heaps made by them, provided they are not fixed or growing, are not solidly embedded and do not adhere to the ball. Sand and loose soil are loose impediments on the putting greens but not elsewhere. Snow and natural ice, other than frost, are either casual water or loose impediments at the option of the player. Man-made ice is an obstruction. Dew and frost are not loose impediments. Except when both the loose impediment and the ball lie in or touch a hazard, any loose impediment may be removed without penalty. If the ball moves, there is no penalty. Casual water is a temporary accumulation of water on the course which is visible before or after the player takes his stance, and is not a water hazard. Dew and frost are not casual water.

Stones in Bunkers

Stones in bunkers are loose impediments in a hazard and therefore under the Rules cannot be moved. In practice, many club committees make a local rule which permits moving such stones, as do most of the professional tours. It is always best to check on the local rules printed on the scorecard.

BALL PLUGGED IN A BUNKER

In a hazard, if a ball is covered by loose impediments or sand, the player may remove as much of it as necessary to enable him to see the ball and identify it. The ball must then be replaced and the lie recreated as near as possible. It is worth putting a distinguishing mark on the ball you are playing so it can be identified in such circumstances.

PUTTING GREEN

The line of a putt must not be touched except: to move sand and loose soil and other loose impediments by picking them up or brushing aside with the hand; in lifting the ball or in measuring a putt; in pressing in a ball-marker; in repairing old hole plugs or ball marks on the green; in removing movable obstructions; in addressing the ball, a player may place the club in front of the ball but without pressing it down. A ball on the green may be lifted and cleaned. The player may not test the surface of the green by rolling a ball or roughening or scraping up the surface. The player shall not make a stroke from a stance astride or with either foot touching the line of the putt or an extension to that line behind the ball. When a ball overhangs the lip of the hole, the player is allowed time to reach the hole without unreasonable delay, plus an additional 10 seconds to determine whether the ball is at rest. If the ball by then has not fallen into the hole, it is deemed to be at rest and must be played.

Ground Under Repair

Ground under repair is any portion of the course so marked by the committee. It includes material piled for removal, and any hole made by a greenkeeper, even if not so marked. Stakes and lines defining ground under repair are included in such ground. The player may lift and drop the ball without penalty at a point on the course nearest to where the ball lay, provided it is not nearer the hole, not interfered with by the ground under repair and not in a hazard or on a putting green.

Out of Bounds

Out of bounds is ground on which play is prohibited. When it is defined by stakes, or a fence, the out of bounds line is determined by the nearest inside points of the stakes or fence posts, excluding angled supports. When defined by a line on the ground, the line itself is out of bounds. The line extends vertically upwards and downwards. The entire ball must be out of bounds. A player may stand out of bounds to play a ball which is in bounds. When a ball is out of bounds, it should be re-played from its original position under penalty of one stroke.

Unplayable Ball

The player may declare his ball unplayable at any place on the course except when the ball lies in or touches a water hazard. The player is the sole judge as to whether his ball is unplayable. If the player deems his ball to be unplayable, under penalty of one stroke, he may: (a) play a ball as nearly as possible at the spot from which the original ball was played; (b) drop a ball within two club-lengths of the spot where the ball lay but not nearer the hole; or (c) drop a ball behind the point where the ball lay, keeping that point directly between the hole and the spot on which the ball is dropped, with no limit to how far behind that point the ball may be dropped. If the unplayable ball is in a bunker, the player may proceed as above except that under clauses (b) or (c) the ball must be dropped in the bunker.

OUTSIDE AGENCY

An outside agency is any agency not part of the match or, in strokeplay, not part of the competitor's side, and includes a referee, a marker, an observer or a forecaddie. Neither wind nor water is an outside agency. A bird or an animal which might disturb the ball is an outside agency.

WINTER RULES

As far as the Rules of Golf are concerned, there is no such thing. However, under temporary local rules designed to 'protect the course or promote fair and pleasant play', one of the things a club committee can do, especially in the winter when conditions may be soft and muddy, is to allow a ball to be moved within six inches to a better lie or lifted out of its own plug mark. It is permitted to clean the ball at the same time. Of course, if you are just out in a friendly fourball, not part of a competition, not returning a card, why not play winter rules? Why not just nudge the ball up on the fairway, it's the same for everybody. Enjoy your golf, move up a tee or two, don't always flog yourself from the back, particularly when you've had a lot of rain and the course is playing long.

Golf is there to be enjoyed! Of course, do play in the club competitions, obeying the rules to the best of your ability, but don't forget there are other ways of enjoying the game amongst friends that hurt nobody.

And what of the world of club golf, the great meeting place of everyone involved in playing this grand game? There have been many changes and, on looking back, the first major change was the introduction of corporate golf. It was somebody's bright idea to approach companies suggesting taking guests/clients/employees for a day's golf, or even an overnight stay. Look at these lovely hotels that have a golf course on their doorstep. A great way to say thank you to your supporters.

Then came the job of who do you ask, what sort of golfing skill (if any) is required before you tackle one of these wonderful adventures. The immediate reaction was it brought in a lot of money for the clubs and hotels where these various events were staged, so from that point of view a lot of people were happy. But suddenly word got round that 18 holes was taking six or seven hours and, on occasion, even more. And so minimum handicaps had to be introduced. Ah, well, you can't please everyone I suppose, but that was the start of it. Money came rolling in and subscriptions were pegged back, but not before some members got fed up with their course being cluttered up with visiting societies three or four days a week.

Having said all that, I loved club life! I was a slow starter; by that I mean being allowed into the clubhouse was a big thing in my young days. In fact the committee at that time at the Ferndown Golf Club waited to see if I was picked for the Ryder Cup team – as if somehow that would have made me more acceptable to go into the club on my own and not at the invitation of one of the members.

Time moves on and now memberships are a bit thin on the

ground. There aren't many clubs with a waiting list. Years ago, some used to be very picky, unless you had a low handicap, worked in a bank or belonged to one of the professions. In those days a 14 or 16 handicapper with a modest job stood very little chance of joining some clubs. Not so today. I think the vast majority would welcome them with open arms, providing they can come up with the necessary entrance fee and subscription. But often these days, with the purse strings tight and other interests and responsibilities pressing, people are less inclined to pay a lump sum up front, not knowing how many rounds they will be able to play during the year. There has been a huge rise in the number of players who simply decide to 'pay and play', when and where they want, and as frequently as time allows. It is up to the clubs to adapt and attract their business.

But all is not doom and gloom, and there are many clubs who survive very well, though most could do with extra income. Even so the internal debates still go on and on, like whether men should be allowed to come into the club with no socks, particularly in the summer time. I wonder why that creates such a fuss?

'Cypress Point is such an exclusive golf club that it had a membership drive and drove out forty members.'
BOB HOPE

What makes a good club? That takes a bit of thinking about. I'm not sure when the first clubs were formed, or why. My guess is that people of like profession and thought decided it would be a good idea to meet, socialise, take meals, quaff wine, or generally do good deeds. Those ideas have been eroded over the years with people wishing to force their way in to either male- or female-dominated clubs for just the hell of it. But for a golf club to be successful you need certain ingredients to get the ball rolling. Firstly, the outdoor staff; you need a knowledgeable, sensible green-keeper with a band of helpers who, in an ideal world, play the game of golf and understand it, so that when they are setting out the tee markers and placing flags, they do so in sensible positions. They need a feel, love and enjoyment of what they're doing, ever trying to improve the quality of the golf course without necessarily bombarding it with chemicals. The nurturing of wildlife and generally creating a feel-good factor out on the course should be part of their brief.

If you get a head green-keeper with those skills, make sure you keep him, in fact make sure he and his team all have decent wages so do not become candidates to be poached away by a neighbouring club. That goes for in-house as well: an ideal steward and staff, a sensible cook, someone who knows how to present a good sandwich or tasty soup, you're not catering for the royal family. Pleasant, smiling staff who take an interest in what they're doing are the key. And a secretary who really enjoys his job and goes out of his way to make sure things work as smoothly as possible.

At the Parkstone we had a wonderful retired bank manager called Bond. No, not James, he was just called Daddy! Why? you ask. Well he had a Swedish wife and two children. Mama, only managing to conquer the English language down to about an 8 handicap, always referred to him as Daddy, so Daddy it was. He was delightful, tall, rather gaunt, a bit untidy, and survived in a small office no more than eight foot by five, which was absolutely chaotic, but he knew where everything was. When anyone complained about anything, whether it was about badly parked cars, the condition of the course or the fact that someone had driven into them at the 14th, it mattered not, the answer was always the same. He listened very patiently and then said, 'I understand, I totally understand, just let me have it in writing and I will place it before the necessary committee.' Well, of course, the complainant huffed and puffed, went home, sat down, had a cup of tea or something stronger and the whole notion of writing letters passed. So the incident ended there and then, with nobody getting irate or demanding that heads should roll. Every club should have a Daddy Bond, but some courses are busier than others and need to be run with military precision.

Gone are the days of retired service personnel taking over a club as a pleasant, rather easy-going job, to supplement their pension. Today modest golf clubs turn over a million pounds or more, which constitutes a formidable business. The big ones turn over several millions, so the days of the retired major have gone, but still, if handled properly, it can be a pleasant vocation. Although some secretaries like to build up their own staff, they change their title from 'Secretary' to 'Chief Executive' and then they have to have a secretary, who in turn has to have an assistant secretary, who in turn has to have an assistant. And so, instead of one slightly harassed Daddy Bond, you have five or six people doing more or less the same job, plus an automated telephone exchange which nobody really understands and most people hate. That's progress?

New legislation over the past few years has brought in many new problems. No more 'slave labour', long hours for little financial reward, but a rewarding job. Now there are rules to be adhered to, health and safety factors, human rights and political correctness. The advent of the drink and drive laws have dented many golf clubs' incomes, especially during the winter months. Somehow in the UK we have not got used to the idea of using a taxi when going out 'on safari'; perhaps it's the cost, perhaps it's just our way. All I know is, golf clubs I pass during the thirty years I've lived on the Surrey/Hampshire borders are now closed around 8 p.m. where once they were filled with people enjoying a drink, snack or having social intercourse up to 10.30 p.m. But I'm sure there are many catering staff who are delighted that this has come to pass!

There's no doubt that golf clubs have become, for want of a better word, more relaxed over the last twenty-five years, for better in the most part, but not always. The American habit of wearing a hat, mainly of a baseball type, indoors, has become a regular feature and one I do not like. Jack Nicklaus, at his magnificent Muirfield Village Golf Club on the outskirts of Cleveland, Ohio, has notices all over the place stating hats will not be tolerated anywhere within the clubhouse.

Changes manifest themselves in many other ways, for example, hardly anyone does any caddying these days. I often wonder why that is. I would have thought a lot of golf clubs would like some juniors to come at weekends and pull a trolley, give them £10 for their trouble, get them interested and generally introduce them to the ways of golf and club life. After all, they may be the members of the future. Years past every golf club I've known had caddies. I can see them now, young urchins who at the bigger clubs were classed as grade 3, the trolley-pullers who tried to follow the flight of the ball but could offer no real advice; grade 2 were a little better; then you got down to the serious brigade, à la Sunningdale, Wentworth, Gleneagles and the like, where every caddie had a story to tell and told it well. They were worth their fee, even if they lost the odd ball or three and left a head cover behind at the 14th!

Such wonderful names. There was Tom the Goose, Fancy Taylor, Swanny, Big Jim, Little Jimmy, Big Charlie, Liverpool Mac, Little Mac, Canada, Tiny Tim, The Colonel, The General (his surname was Lee, so that was simple). And then there was Mad Mac, one of the great characters at Sunningdale. He sometimes caddied for Max Faulkner who won the Open Championship at Royal Portrush in 1951. It was said his brother was an air commodore but we never had proof of that. He'd been badly affected by the war. Today there would be 'counselling'. Round his neck hung a pair of opera glasses with no lenses! When caddying he used to lie full length on the green, examine the line through the glasses end to end, then solemnly announce, 'It's slightly straight, guv'nor.' He travelled everywhere with an old hickory-shafted club with no grip, but bound with miles of string, twine, raffia and the like until it was as thick as a cricket bat. He'd been known to place a ball in Piccadilly Circus and knock it up to Leicester Square – well, there wasn't much traffic in those days!

10

HOW TO STAY FIT FOR GOLF

'Golfers find it a very trying matter to turn at the waist,
more particularly if they have a lot of waist to turn.'
HARRY VARDON

Age is an exacting master. If you're lucky you're sailing along doing pretty well the same things as you used to do twenty-five years before, when suddenly you notice a stiffening in the joints. The looseness in the arms, wrists and hands isn't quite the same, but there's nothing to be done about it except, hopefully, to grow old gracefully and as intelligently as we possibly can.

Of course, golf of itself is a good form of exercise, especially for the more mature person. But what about being 'fit for golf'? In all honesty, over the years you could not confuse golfers with trained athletes, not with all those bulging waistlines around. It was generally felt that if your hands were strong and your legs could carry you round 36 holes in a day, that would be quite enough for golf fitness. In their time, powerful players such as Arnold Palmer and Jack Nicklaus did little other than play golf to maintain their strength.

There were exceptions, of course, and Gary Player was the leader of the pack doing all sorts of exercises. He was also a runner, as was Bob Charles, and it must have contributed to their wonderful longevity as golfers at the highest level. And Sam Snead was so super-supple he could kick the lintel above a door. Not something I'd recommend you to do in your advanced years but what *can* you do? Henry Cotton used to squeeze a little rubber ball to strengthen the wrists and hands and you can buy a little hand exerciser which does the same job. As well as strong hands, strong legs are very important in golf, so anything that builds stamina can only help. And if you are carrying a few extra pounds? Well, as long as you are enjoying life what is the harm, but if you can shed the odd pound it will be less strain on the legs and that can only help your golf.

Looking at the professional scene today, there are still golfers around of the more rotund persuasion, but Tiger Woods has led the way in showing how important fitness is at the highest level. They say that he could have succeeded at any athletic pastime that took his fancy. However, it is not just his all-round fitness that helps his swing, but also his ability to concentrate under intense pressure, in hot and humid conditions, perhaps with jet-lag after flying in from the other side of the world, so that he can perform exactly as he desires on the 18th hole as well as the 1st.

A coterie of young players follow in his footsteps on the treadmill as well as the fairways, wonderfully lithe young men like Colombia's Camilo Villegas. But there can be a price to be paid and the busiest place at a golf tournament these days is probably the physiotherapy unit. All sorts of tweaks need the magic treatment. Bad backs are traditionally the golfer's curse, but it is worrying when a young player like Justin Rose keeps having trouble. Then there is Tiger's left knee. He has already had three operations on it, the latest just days after the 2008 Masters which meant that the next time he walked eighteen holes was in the first round of the US Open at Torrey Pines. He won in a sensational manner, but at what cost?

But it is not just the professionals who suffer from injuries. Perhaps not surprisingly, amateur players, who are less prepared physically, also get injured. I am indebted to leading physiotherapist Elizabeth Sharp, ESPH, 22 Harley Street, London W1G 9PL, who specialises in helping athletes, and to her colleague Darren Norman, for explaining the most common injuries and offering some basic exercises to keep you in trim. It is not a question of becoming a bore about training but you might be surprised how doing a few things to build up problem areas or sticking to a general plan can help you enjoy your golf more. If you have any queries about your general health, you should first seek advice from your doctor.

Golf injuries are common in both the professional and the amateur golfer. The vast majority of golf injuries are not the result of single accidents but occur as the result of tissue injury sustained from overuse or poor posture:

A survey of 1,000 amateur golfers revealed that:

- More than 60 per cent sustained a golf-related injury at some point in their career.
- Incidence of injury was higher in amateur players over the age of fifty (65 per cent injury rate).
- Injury rate was similar for male and female golfers.
- Injury led amateur golfers to miss five weeks a year of play per person per year on average.

Common causes of injury reported amongst amateur golfers include:

- No warm up.

- Poor swing mechanics.
- Hitting the ground or an object during a swing.
- Excessive play or practice.

Common areas of injury include:

- Lower back 35 per cent, elbow 33 per cent, wrist/hand 20 per cent, shoulder 12 per cent, knee 9 per cent.

Key points:

- Injuries are often the result of overuse and poor posture.
- Prevalence of injuries amongst amateur golfers is very high.
- Injuries to the lower back are very common in amateur golfers.
- Injuries to the upper limbs account for more than 50 per cent of all injuries.

GENERAL WARM-UP

Walk either round the car park or around the club facilities for three to five minutes to warm the muscles and get the blood and oxygen circulating around the body.

HOW TO PREVENT BACK INJURIES

1 Rotate the shoulder and hip about the same amount during the backswing.
2 Keep the spine vertical and avoid over-extending the lumbar spine on follow through.
3 Reducing stiffness between the shoulder blades will improve the ability of the body to recoil during the golf swing, dramatically increasing the potential power you can generate and subsequently the distances that you may potentially hit the ball.
4 Improve your core stability and strengthen your back muscles.

BACK EXERCISES

Side bending

Stand with feet apart and even weight on both feet. Hold a club in your hands above your head. Bend as far as you can to the left and then to the right. Keep your tummy flat and do not overstretch.

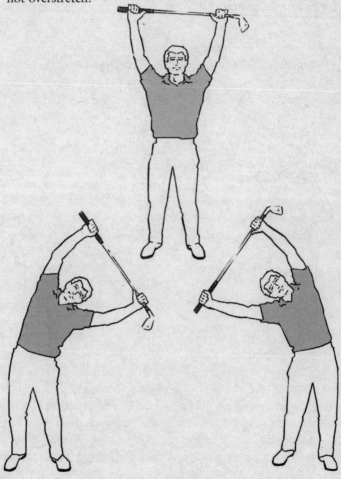

Back rotation

Stand with feet apart and even weight on both feet. Hold a club in both hands behind your head. Make sure that you keep your head upright and do not push your neck forwards. Twist your body to the right as far as you can and then to the left. Keep your feet flat on the ground and keep your tummy flat. Do five to ten swings.

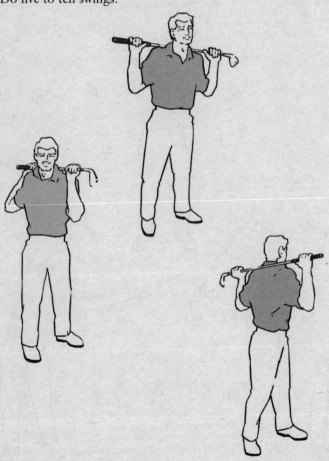

Upper back (thoracic) rotation

Put one hand on the boot of your car or on a tree or flat surface. Lean down so that your back is almost flat. Keep your feet flat on the ground and apart. Swing your other arm like a pendant across your body and upwards to rotate your upper body. Keep your head down. Do five to ten swings and then repeat with the other arm.

Back stretch

Stand with feet apart. Draw your lower tummy muscles in and slowly stretch your hands down the front of your thighs curling down each spinal vertebra one at a time until your hands are as near to your toes as possible. If your hamstring muscles at the back of your thighs are too tight bend your knees slightly. Uncurl back up to the upright position slowly one vertebra at a time. Repeat three times.

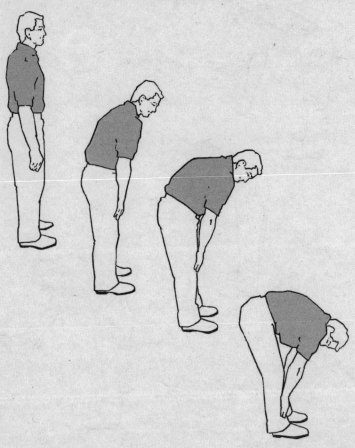

Core stability to maintain support for the back

Keep the lumbar spine and pelvis in neutral alignment at all times to prevent back injury. Activate the deep abdominal muscle, transversus abdominus, which flattens the lower abdomen below the tummy button. This is particularly important in the backswing to prevent over-extension of the lower back which can compress the lower vertebrae and cause back pain.

SPINAL ALIGNMENT AND POSTURE

Spinal alignment and posture are vital to prevent poor biomechanics and damage to the spine. The spine needs to be in a neutral position to maintain equilibrium.

Tip your pelvis up at the front so that your back feels flatter. This will activate the transversus abdominus muscle at the front of your abdomen. The action of this muscle is to draw the lower abdomen flat and thereby improve stability, support and strength for the back.

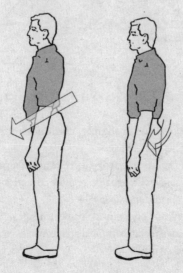

ABDOMINAL (TUMMY) MUSCLE STRENGTHENING

Leg slides (home exercise)

Lie on your back with both hips and knee bent and feet flat on the floor. Tilt your pelvis towards your ribs so that you can feel your spine gently against the floor. Activate the lower abdominal muscle breathing normally. Slowly slide your right leg down the floor keeping your back flat. Slide back up to the start position and repeat with the left leg. Do five leg slides on alternate legs.

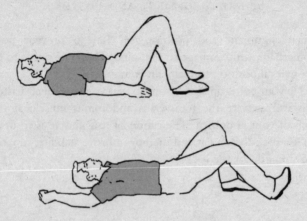

HOW TO PREVENT SHOULDER INJURIES

1 Shorten the backswing slightly, ending with the club at one o'clock on the backswing.
2 Strengthen your rotator cuff and scapular muscles effectively. This will greatly reduce the risk of overstrain around the shoulder.
3 Strengthen your chest and back muscles, including the pectorals and the latissimus dorsi muscles which generate power in the swing.

SHOULDER EXERCISES

Shoulder rotator cuff exercise

The rotator cuff muscles are small and deep inside the shoulder joint. They are very important muscles that keep the ball of the arm bone, the humerus, centralised in the socket of the shoulder joint. If they are not working correctly the shoulder may become painful.

Sit or stand. Put your hands and elbows together and lift your elbows to shoulder height. Keeping elbows to fingertip in contact, take your hands to the right as far as you can and then to the left as far as you can. You should feel a stretch at the back of your shoulder.

Shoulder rolls

Put your fingertips on your shoulders. Circle your elbows round from front to back without shrugging up towards your ears. You should feel the muscles above your shoulders warm up and relax as the blood flow increases. Roll your shoulders ten times.

HOW TO PREVENT NECK INJURIES

Neck exercises

Stand with feet apart and shoulders down. Tilt your head to the right, taking your ear towards your shoulder and then tilt to the left side. Tilt right and left five times.

Then turn your head to the right and left as far as you can. Keep your shoulders still. Turn right and left five times.

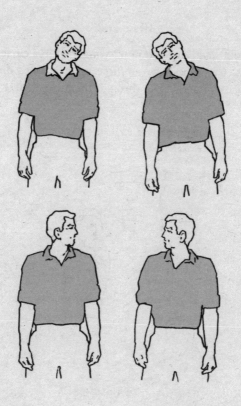

HOW TO PREVENT WRIST, ELBOW AND FOREARM INJURIES

1 Take advice on size and type of club grip and the correct club length to suit you.
2 Select irons with graphite shafts, large heads and 'sweet-spots' to lessen vibration.
3 Strengthen the forearm muscles and keep them flexible.

Wrist circles

Stretch your hand out and move your wrist in a circle in both directions. Circle both wrists three times in both directions. Keep your shoulders down through the movement.

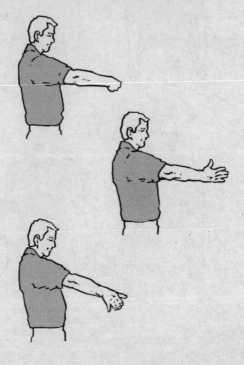

Wrist stretches

Put your hands together, making sure that they are in contact all the time from the heel of your hand to the tips of your fingers. Press your hands down towards your waist with fingertips pointing upwards. Then rotate your fingertips down to face the ground. Keep your shoulders down through the movement. Repeat five times up and down.

Forearm stretches

Straighten your arm in front of you and with your palm facing away from you bend the wrist and fingers back with the other hand to stretch the muscles on the front of your forearm. Then turn your palm to face towards you and stretch the back of your wrist and the muscles on the back of your forearm. Keep your shoulders down throughout the movement. Hold for five seconds and repeat twice in both directions.

HIP AND KNEE STRENGTHENING

Knee dips

Stand on one leg and bend your support knee as far as you can without lifting your heel. Stand tall with your deep tummy muscles activated and pelvis and shoulders in a neutral position. Repeat five times on each leg.

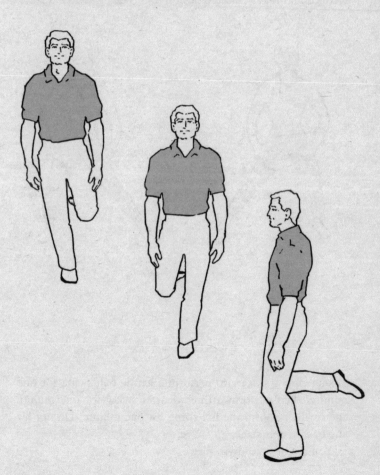

Knee lunges with inside thigh stretch

Stand with feet about four feet apart and toes facing forwards. Bend the right knee as far as you can without lifting your foot and feel the quadriceps muscle at the front of your knee working and the adductor muscle in the inside of your left thigh being stretched. Repeat on the left side. Hold for twenty seconds and repeat three times on each side.

SWING PRACTICE

Take a club and start to perform a gentle half swing for one minute, then perform a three-quarter swing for one minute and finally perform the full swing for one minute. Do not hit any balls at this stage.

You are now ready to play.

No one enjoys playing golf more than Arnold Palmer, who led the game into the television age in America in the 1950s and '60s. Palmer still loves to play games with friends, or anyone really, but finally gave up playing competitively after his fiftieth consecutive appearance in the Masters tournament at Augusta. This year, 2008, Gary Player beat Arnie's record by playing in his fifty-first Masters (not all consecutively, as he had to miss one year due to an operation). At the age of seventy-one, Gary has often 'shot his age' in competition, that is scoring at or below his age, but at Augusta he knew he was not going to make the cut and qualify for the last two rounds over the weekend. But that did not stop him doing what he has done all his career, setting himself a goal to try to attain. He said if he could break 80, he would return for a fifty-second appearance and he managed it with a little room to spare. So dedicated has Player been to fitness and making the very best of himself that it is hard to see him ever stopping. His impact on the tournament did not stop there. In a voice message to the 54-hole leader, his young countryman Trevor Immelman, on the Saturday night – typically Gary was flying off to the Middle East to look in on some design project he has there – he said simply he knew Trevor would win the next day and offered some sage advice. Gary's enthusiasm is infectious and Immelman used the message as an inspiration on his way to victory.

Without Palmer, the Seniors Tour in the States, for those aged fifty and over, would not have got off the ground. Arnie's Army simply could not get enough of him and the new circuit, the Champions Tour, has led to many of the great players extending their careers. Player, of course, thrived, as did Lee Trevino, Bob Charles, Jack Nicklaus and Hale Irwin. Today, Loren Roberts and Jay Haas, neither of whom quite managed to win a major championship on the regular tour, enjoy great success, while Bernhard Langer, who was one of

Europe's big five from the 1980s – Ballesteros, Faldo, Woosnam, Lyle and Langer – has kept his game and health in excellent shape and has had a spectacular debut.

> *'Why should I play with the flat-bellies when I can play with the round-bellies?'*
> LEE TREVINO confirming his intention to leave the main US Tour and join the senior circuit in 1989.

When the European Senior Tour came along, Neil Coles, who hated flying and never made it in America, proved that it was perfectly possible to maintain a high standard over an amazingly long time by winning in six decades. My friend and old Ryder Cup partner Christy O'Connor Snr was another who played fine golf late into his career. He was a fairly late developer, not winning an important event in Britain until he was in his thirties. That hurdle overcome in 1955, he remained one of the top players in Europe for over fifteen years. After that he confined himself to pro-ams and his annual appearance in the Irish Open, in which he finished joint third in 1982. Before the European Senior Tour arrived there was only the PGA Seniors Championship and Christy dominated, winning six times in eight years against players a good deal younger.

Christy had his aches and pains, so how is it that his game lasted so well? What lessons can we learn from his game? Well, of course, Christy was a genius at the game and blessed with an exceptionally relaxed swing. He used to say that he had to limit himself to a just few loosener shots before going out to play a tournament round. If he went through a full practice routine, he became too relaxed and his play suffered. Relaxation in the swing was the key to his continuing success. As we grow older, it is even more important to keep tension out. Inevitably we become less supple, and if we are tense as well, our golf swing will soon become short, jerky and snatchy.

Above Prestwick, on the Ayrshire coast, epitomises the austere majesty of links golf.

Below When the rhododendrons are in flower, what better place is there to be than the Duke's Course at Woburn.

Above It's the results that matter – Bernhard Langer (*left*) displays his unique putting grip, and Ian Woosnam (*right*) wields a long-handled putter.

Royal Lytham and St Annes is high on my list of all-time favourite places.

Above Ernie Els is one of the most accomplished bunker players I have ever seen.

Above Monty in full flow is a superb striker of the ball.

Below Intimidating it may be but we spent many happy hours at Gleneagles filming *Pro-Celebrity Golf.*

Sandy Lyle is one of the most natural players of all time.

Right Laura Davies has been one of Britain's finest lady golfers for many years.

Below This may look like the first golf course on the moon but in fact it's Royal St George's, Sandwich, a lovely course.

Above A wounded Tiger proved highly dangerous, winning the 2008 US Open despite a serious knee problem.

Above Greg Norman during his remarkable performance in the 2008 Open – it's never too late.

Below Annika Sorensen has set new standards for women's golf.

Early in his career, Tiger Woods shows all his powerful elegance.

Right No longer a grumpy old man.

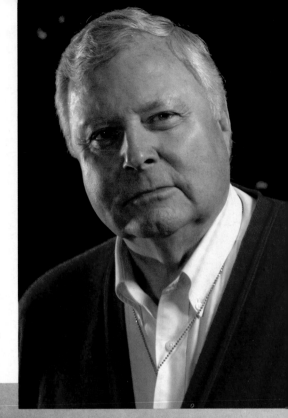

Below Two generations of Ryder Cup golfers. My father, Percy, was one of the greatest iron players.

So try to follow O'Connor. By all means grip the club firmly but not so firm that your forearm muscles and shoulders feel tight, then swing back easily, making sure you complete the backswing and begin the downswing in as leisurely a way as you can. Make sure you do those simple exercises and movements.

Other examples must include Ben Hogan, who once despaired of ever earning a living as a professional golfer but went on to become one of its greatest players. It took him years to build a swing on which he could rely. He did not feel he had found the secret of being able to hit full out without fearing the hook until 1948, when he was thirty-six. A year later he almost lost his life in a car accident but battled back to become an even better player than he was before, and in 1953 won each of the three major championships in which he played.

Sam Snead holds the record for winning on the US Tour at the age of fifty-two. He had been the first player regularly to drive the ball over 300 yards and at the age of sixty-two he finished joint third in a major championship. At the age of seventy-two he was still earning a living on the Seniors Tour. Snead was exceptionally flexible. Well past middle age, Snead could do high kicks above his head. Some golfers are not really flexible enough to swing back as far as the horizontal without letting go with either fingers or wrists, but Snead could swing back as far as he liked. Backswing inevitably shortens with age, but this was no problem for Snead: he had suppleness in plenty to spare.

Roberto de Vicenzo was another who had a majestic swing and could seemingly go on and on. Roberto performed well in the Open Championship when past his mid-fifties and on the US Seniors Tour into his sixties. He always vastly enjoyed practice, the lonely joy of hitting and watching it fly, another vital element in continuing success, at whatever level, in golf for those no longer young. Without enthusiasm you are lost.

Many when they find they are not playing as well as they used to, just give up. I suspect that in a spell of poor form they become confused. They don't realise that it may only be a temporary falling off. Instead, they come to believe that the ageing process is to blame, rather than poor technique. This book is precisely for those people. It's time to seek advice, not to give up.

11

HOW TO THINK BETTER GOLF

'Water creates a neurosis in golfers. The very thought of this harmless fluid robs them of their normal powers of rational thought, turns their legs to jelly, and produces a palsy of the upper limbs.'

PETER DOBEREINER, *The Glorious World of Golf*, 1973

Nothing pleases a Grumpy Old Man more than out-foxing a young, flashy newcomer. As we have seen, power is not the main weapon of the mature golfer – it is experience and cunning. It is all about thinking your way to success, not whizzing to the first tee and thrashing the biggest-faced driver you can find as hard as you dare. Oh, no!

There was no more cerebral golfer than the Australian Peter Thomson. If ever his game was off, he would head not for the course or the practice range but an armchair. When he had worked out what was causing the problem, he would hit no more than a handful of shots on the practice ground to confirm the diagnosis and then would be ready for his next round. He was often outdriven by most of his opponents but it never worried him. He said, 'The most important facets of golf are careful planning, calm and clear thinking and the ordinary logic of common sense. Golf calls for logical observation. Beyond that the big thing is not power but judgment.'

It amazes me that captains of industry, senior executives and managers completely ignore what made them successful in business as soon as they step on to a golf course. If they managed their business as they played golf, they would be out of a job. But if they applied their management skills – planning ahead, setting a budget, weighing the risks, thinking positively – then their handicap could come tumbling down by as much as ten strokes.

The right mental approach begins long before you get to your golf club. Gary Player thought it started the night before. He said he never went to dinner with poor putters because he didn't want to spend the evening hearing about all the putts they had missed. Instead, he went out with good putters so that he could pick up good vibes by hearing about all the putts they holed. Now, if you can't ask Ben Crenshaw, Brad Faxon, Seve Ballesteros and Tiger Woods round for dinner, where do you start? Let's look at your equipment. Are your grips dry? Have you cleaned them recently to get back the tackiness and remove the shine? What are your shoes like? Have you dried them out in a cool dry place (not on a radiator!) if they were soaked through last time out? Are spikes missing or too worn down to grip, assuming you don't have soft spikes? If so, get to your pro's shop early and have replacements fitted.

A look at the faces of your irons is always worth the trouble. Are the grooves filled with hard dried mud and grass? Although this makes little difference to backspin, everyone *feels* more of a golfer when using a new ball and setting a gleaming clubface against it. It helps to give you confidence, the lack of which is a prime cause of many bad rounds.

Finally, think about your clothing. See what the weathermen have to say and plan your day's outfit so that you can keep yourself and your clubs dry. Both winter and summer temperatures can change a great deal in the course of a day and winds suddenly rise or fall. No professional worth his salt sets out in a tournament without a spare sweater or two, an umbrella and a reliable set of waterproofs. Some kind of headgear is also essential. None of us likes the feeling of rain trickling down the neck from a rain-soaked head.

Of course, when temperatures rise, storm clouds often give way to hot, humid afternoons. You should always be able to strip down to something both comfortable and acceptable to your club – perhaps a cotton shirt. A small pot of suncream can also come in handy if the sun actually comes out.

These minor, but highly important, things accomplished, you are ready to set out, and I hope you've allowed yourself plenty of time. It doesn't help produce a relaxed swing on the first tee if you have had to fight a losing battle on the way, with every traffic light set at red and every car in front of you apparently on a leisurely sight-seeing excursion. It is much better to arrive for a game with a reasonable amount of time to spare. If you are playing at your home club, this need only be ten minutes or so. If, however, you are due at a strange venue, bear in mind that most golf clubs are not well signposted. You may have to stop a couple of times to ask directions, and you will also need time to solve the geography of the clubhouse once you have arrived.

One more purchase at the pro's shop could be vital. There is a reason they call it a 'strokesaver'. These maps of the course have all the yardages marked, note all the hazards and such like, and are a great help if you have never played the course before. Even on your home course, you can use it to make your own notes on hazards that cause you particular trouble. Of course, knowing these yardages – and being aware of 150-yard markers on the course and yardages on sprinkler heads – only helps if you know how far you hit each club. This is one of the key things you should establish when practising on the driving range. It is the basis of being able to implement sensible course management, which, as Peter Thomson suggests, is the key to putting together a good score. Once the basics of the game are understood, 90 per cent of the game is to do with judgment and attitude. The trouble with the vast majority of golfers is that they think only about improving the 10 per cent that is concerned with improving your swing and chipping and putting. All golfers can improve the management of their game and it would be a revelation to play a round with your local professional, asking him to advise you on what shot to play, what club to use and the like, and not worry about anything technical.

So, here you are on the first tee, ready for your playing lesson. You are now about to play one of the most important shots of your golfing day. Not many courses start with a par-three, so you will probably need to use a wooden club for your first shot. Success or failure at this point can have a very strong influence on your confidence in the rest of the round. So give yourself every chance and use a club you trust. If it's your driver, fine, but if you feel safer with a three- or four-wood (even a five-iron), use that. For most of us, the choice will probably be a wood with some loft on the face. If in the end you hit a shot with some slice or hook on it, the loft will help to prevent a disaster.

For the first shot of the round, be sure that you *complete* your backswing (nothing hurried and jerky please!) and that you swing freely through the ball, your main thought being to make solid contact. If you manage these two things, your

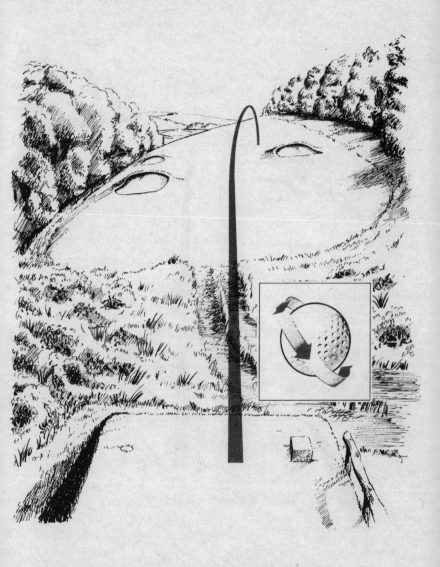

The flight pattern of a drive fading left to right and holding on a right-to-left-sloping fairway

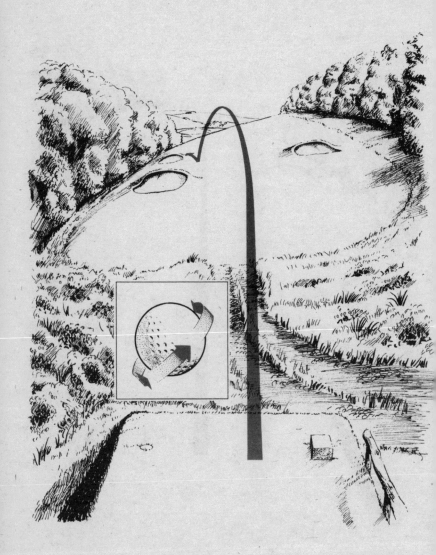

This flight pattern shows the ball moving right to left on a right-to-left slope and disappearing into trouble

chances of making a successful shot are quite high; slim or none if you jerk the club quickly away, hurry it back down and are all anxiety in the hitting area, ready to look up to see what disaster has befallen you.

Good, that wasn't bad at all, was it? You carried out my basic demands well enough. Perhaps the clubface was a little open or shut, but your ball is on the fairway, a respectable distance away.

Let's suppose you are now faced with a second shot to a flag some 180 yards away in the middle of a green. Even if you are a fair long-iron player, now is not the time to take one out of your bag unless you've given yourself some time on the practice ground and are full of confidence. Far better to use a club with which you don't need to hit flat out, so you can concentrate on swinging easily but firmly and getting the clubhead to meet the back of the ball.

'I'll be through the back of the green,' did I hear you say? Well, possibly, but it's early in your round and your muscles won't have loosened up, so that's unlikely. Even if you do go through, consider how much trouble there is on the approach. Most golf holes are designed with bunkers to catch and slopes to divert inaccurate approach shots. Sometimes going through a green gives less of a penalty than being short. However, ignore my advice about over-clubbing if there's a river, ravine or impenetrable bushes immediately behind!

Ah, you struck that one moderately well, though nothing fancy. It was a little off line but almost exactly the right length. You've got a twenty-foot putt from the left edge. So far, your confidence ought to be building nicely. You have attempted nothing spectacular (your opponent, who tried to boom a drive off the first tee, half-topped it and then tried to crack a three-iron out of the rough, has just reached the green in four) and you've done nothing very wrong.

See how much room there is behind the flag at the back of the green and on the apron

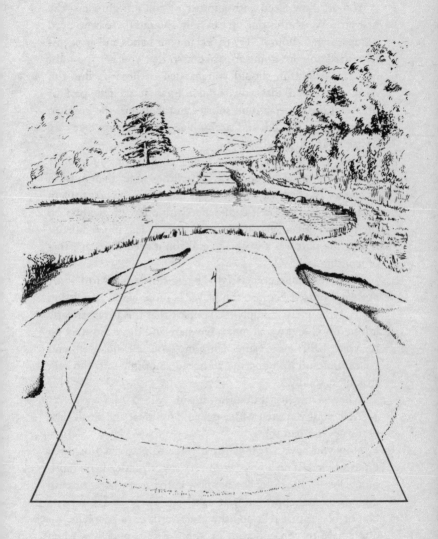

You are now faced with another of golf's frighteners: the first putt. Weigh this one up carefully, though there is no need to take an age about it. Try to feel in your hands and arms just how hard you are going to strike it so that you get the right length. Delightful, should you happen to hole it. But I'm more concerned that you shouldn't rap it six feet past or dribble it the same amount short – and then miss the next. So concentrate on length and strength and let direction take care of itself – it usually does.

Well, not bad, you gave the hole a chance but you're three feet past. But, alas, three feet is still a little longer than most of us like for the first 'easy' putt of the day. It will be no problem if you've given yourself confidence with a few great putts on the practice green, but it will look a great deal more difficult if your last putt was a week ago and you missed from that sort of length.

What you must now avoid is being too tense. Most short putts are missed because the player is more afraid of missing than anything else. Simply tell yourself that this is rather early in the round and we all miss a few here and there. So walk up to your ball, make sure you line yourself up well and concentrate on bringing the clubhead smoothly into the ball, striking it solidly.

Whew! Only just, but a least it's in.

Well, you've started with a par, and for great and small alike that's never a bad thing.

Now you have a 150-yard par-three to play. Two or three times a year you hit a seven-iron very sweetly indeed and finish quite close to the hole. You are now in the area where the club golfer's mental approach is at its worst. There by the tee is a box or board that tells you the exact yardage (a problem you don't have to contend with on the par-fours and fives when playing your shot to the green). You will be apt to think that you 'ought' to play this particular par-three with a certain club, especially if you are in a fourball and all the others pull out the same club because they are thinking the same thing. But there's at least a club's difference between a shot on a hot day when the air is thin and the same shot when humidity is high. Many players, however, will take out the same club for a winter's day with the air heavy and the ground soggy as they would do in thin air with the ground hard and running. So think about these things and don't allow thoughts of what the other fellow is using or what you 'ought' to be able to reach with to intrude. Even with no wind whatsoever, weather conditions can mean the difference between a nine- or eight-iron and perhaps even a four.

Above all, remember that the name of the game on a par-three is hitting the ball on to the green, and better still, near the hole. What club you use matters not in the least.

Let me illustrate this with a Christy O'Connor story. He was once playing a par-three with a young muscular up-and-comer. O'Connor coasted in a high left-to-right drifter quite near the flag. Your up-and-comer responded with a low rasping drawn eight-iron that finished an equal distance away and then asked, 'What did you use?' 'A five,' O'Connor replied. 'Oh, I only needed an eight,' replied the young man, highly pleased with himself and perhaps also feeling that Christy was rather getting on in years, no longer able to crack a ball away with all the exuberance of his youth.

O'Connor decided to give the young man the lesson that a shot to a green is about getting the ball on the green – never mind what club you do it with. He proceeded to tip a collection of golf balls out of his bag and then sent all of them on to the green with every club in the bag, varying his shot-making from a hooded low wedge to, in the end, a high-drifting driver shot. 'That's what it's all about,' said Christy at the end of this demonstration. I don't know if the lesson was earned, but it was certainly well taught.

So my message is: use the club that will get you pin high if you hit it somewhere near the middle with a reasonable swing – not the one that will require a perfect shot. Remember, the holes with odd pars – the threes and the fives – are your scoring holes. It should be possible to hit the green in regulation figures and then two-putt for your par. At a par-three you have the advantage of playing your approach shot from the teeing ground, while on a par-five you will have a 'spare' shot with which to recover if you get out of position. It is on the long holes that you should be looking to lay up so that you have a wedge shot or a short-iron with which to approach the green. On the par-fours, especially the longer ones, you may also want to lay up rather than force yourself to hit a very long approach because you think you ought to be on the green in two shots. Instead, you probably don't hit the shot very well and end up in more trouble, perhaps taking a double bogey or worse. Again, if it is a case of hitting your Sunday best to get over a hazard, you are far better off playing the percentages rather than 'going for glory'. A sensible lay-up shot would allow you to hit a short approach shot, giving yourself the chance to one-putt for a par or two-putt for a bogey – or rather a net par if you have a 'shot'. That's how to use your handicap allowance intelligently.

Now golf would be very boring if you always hit the ball the same distances on the same hole every time. But it is an outdoor activity and the conditions do come into play, as we discussed earlier. The first factor to take into account is the wind, which is often changing constantly, especially on the great British links courses. If you have to play into a headwind, try to keep the ball low (if it balloons up it will slice or hook more severely) and expect very little roll. So take a stronger club than you normally would, grip a little down it, set the hands forward of the clubhead and hit the ball with a three-quarter punch. Instead of trying to hit the ball harder than ever to get through the wind, remember the old adage: 'Swing easy in the wind' – and think of Ernie Els, known as the 'Big Easy' for his smooth swing, winning the Open at Muirfield in 2002.

Downwind, you also must try not to slam the ball extra hard. You should tee it well up and make a full, smooth swing, letting the wind do the work. Take into account that you will gain extra distance (so check again where the hazards are) plus accuracy, as the wind tends to straighten out a slice or hook.

Crosswinds can be very contrary. A left-to-righter is not too bad for the hook: you can aim straight where you want to end up and let the wind straighten it out. But if you slice, you have to aim off well left and try to keep the ball low to avoid too much wind drift. With a right-to-left wind, the reverse is true. The habitual slicer can for once aim straight, as his slice will fight the wind and he may even hit the ball farther. The hooker should aim right, again punching the ball with a three-quarter swing to keep it low under the wind. One more thing: if you are not entirely sure of the effect of the wind strength or direction, it's not much good tossing bits of grass in the air when you're standing on the tee. Look at the trees down the course instead: don't forget, the ball will rise at least to treetop height.

On the fairway, there is the additional complication of the lie of the ball. This can really influence direction, something many club golfers, despite having played for years, fail to appreciate. If you are standing with your right foot above your left on a downhill lie, you need to select a more lofted club as, for example, a six-iron will play more like a five-iron, the slope cancelling out some of the loft. You then need to keep your weight on your left side, play the ball more off your right foot and aim left of the target. On an uphill lie, you have the reverse situation. You must take a less lofted club, lean into the slope and play the ball nearer your left foot, so that the club strikes it at the bottom of the arc, and aim right of the target.

On a sidehill lie, when the ball is below your feet, it will tend to slice. So you just set up aiming left, standing close with a full-length grip and your weight slightly back on your heels. If the ball is above your feet it will tend to hook. So stand a little farther from the ball, grip down the shaft, weight on the balls of your feet and aim right of the target. With all these shots, don't be too ambitious with length. You must avoid lunging at the ball at all costs and losing your balance. You should also take a few practice swings in situ, just to get the feel of how you should balance and swing.

Back at our playing lesson, if all is going well, and you are playing to your handicap, then your confidence is rising, and confidence is mainly what golf is all about. Any player who believes he is about to hit a good shot, his mind blank to thoughts of failure, is halfway there.

But let's suppose that you followed my advice as best you could but the results were, well, rather frightening. You took a four-wood from the first tee, which was very sensible, but hit behind the ball and achieved a distance of about 100 yards. You then took out your 'safest' club, the five-iron, and half-topped that one another seventy-five yards. Obviously, whatever confidence you began with has withered away by now. Yet you must still think positively.

This is the time, in fact, when you ought to remind yourself that golf is quite a difficult game. Those two horrible shots were really only half an inch away from being quite good ones. The next one is quite likely to be much better. I know from experience that so many club golfers virtually abandon the day if they begin badly. But this is rather silly. Look at the professionals. I remember Nick Faldo once starting a round in the Open with a couple of sixes (to be four over par), a start that no club golfer, however high his handicap, could possibly take encouragement from. But Faldo managed to finish in 68. At a very different level, there was a club golfer, playing off a

10 handicap, who began his round on Captain's Day with an 11 on the first hole, a par-three. Eight of his strokes had gone in the first five minutes. Yet Alan Telford, the 10-handicapper, had the rare ability to look at each shot as a separate matter. Of course, he wasn't in the least pleased by his 11, but at the second he was able to put the disaster out of his mind. He birdied the hole, made few errors in the rest of his round, and eventually finished with a net 67, good enough to win the competition.

But remember, in golf, perhaps in more than any other game, luck does come into the equation. The early part of 2008 saw two outrageous pieces of luck, one good, one bad. Kenny Perry, who was involved in a playoff against the young Japanese Ryuji Imada, played his second at the first playoff hole and it was heading right of the green but should have been okay. Then the ball hit a solitary tree, ricocheted straight across the green into a water hazard, and that was that. His opponent struggled to get a par-five but won first prize. The reverse of that was Richard Finch, when winning the Irish Open at Adair Manor in southern Ireland. He was two shots ahead playing the last hole but pushed his tee shot into the rough. (I know the nerve ends must have been jangling.) He hit his recovery shot too far, the ball went across the fairway and was very lucky to stop short of the water hazard, but on a steep bank. From there he risked all, hoicking it round, on to the green some 100 yards away, ending up at least thirty-five yards from the hole. Understandably he three-putted, to claim victory, but he committed two poor, unthinking errors and got away with it. Perry hardly did anything wrong, and lost out. Those sorts of situation enter into the world of sport many times and at many levels.

Most club golfers are a little more dogged and persistent in matchplay than they are in a stroke competition. But there are situations in which nearly all of us would give up. A friend of mine, the late Michael Hobbs, bored me more than once with a blow-by-blow account of a singles match he played in his club knockout nearly fifty years ago. It went something like this, as I remember.

Going to the 11th tee, Michael was eight-down with eight holes left to play. He had not been playing particularly badly, but his opponent was way above his normal game. Then came a remarkable swing as the form of the two players went into reverse. Michael began to get all the pars and birdies, while his opponent played steadily enough off his 16 handicap but dropped a shot a hole, or matched his par against a Hobbs birdie.

Well, they finished all square on the 18th and there was no club rule governing procedure for the competition. Should they play sudden death or come back and fight another day over a full round? Of course, Michael was bursting with confidence, whereas his opponent's game had fallen to pieces as the unthinkable had come nearer and nearer to reality. Foolishly Michael agreed to a rematch, when his psychological advantage in sudden death would have been overwhelming. However, what happened later (he lost!) is beside the point. The lesson is that very strange turn-arounds can happen at golf. Never give up.

Let me give you an example from my own career. Strangely enough, though I won more than twenty major events, I never managed to win the Matchplay Championship. But in the Ryder Cup I learned a great deal about the matchplay mental game and the importance of not giving up.

My Ryder Cup career eventually came to an end. In it I had played some of my finest golf, exalted by the occasion, the flag-raising ceremony with the bands playing, we Davids against the Goliaths. So, although I never won the Matchplay Championship, after a poor start, I lost my fear of matchplay golf. Today, I consider it the finest form of the game, though many professionals dislike it. They hate the finality of being beaten in the first round and prefer strokeplay events where, after a fairly poor start, they can still produce a string of 66s and take the prize.

In matchplay golf, as when playing a medal, the right mental approach is essential. Remember these key thoughts and you won't go too far wrong:

Don't try extra hard to beat your opponent. Let him beat himself. Losing a hole to a bogey is a no-no; force him to make pars and, hopefully, birdies.

Remember that mistakes will happen, short putts will be missed. But in matchplay the worst that can happen is that you lose one hole. By the time you get to the next tee, forget what happened and focus on the hole in front of you.

Don't worry about being out-driven by a bigger hitter. If you are playing your approach shots first, then you have the chance to put the pressure on him by hitting your ball close to the hole.

Never give up, it's amazing how matches can turn around. Remember the hardest hole to win is the one to clinch the match, so make your opponent work until the very end.

And remember, golf is a game where brain beats brawn.

12

HOLIDAY BREAKS

'A fine spring day at St George's, with the larks singing as they seem to sing nowhere else; the sun is shining on the waters of Pegwell Bay and lighting up the white cliffs in the distance.'
BERNARD DARWIN, golf writer

Now let's assume you have invested some time and a little money in this wondrous world of golf and you find you're enjoying it, indeed you've made amazing progress and in the space of a couple of years maximum, you're playing off a handicap of 18 or 20. You've also made several golfing friends and the conversation has got around to, 'What about going away for a few days' golf?' A very commendable idea but it does take some planning.

Over the last few years several new holiday destinations have opened up which have created a lot of interest, not only because of their good weather but the first-class value of the golfing packages. I shouldn't be surprised if this doesn't change again over the next few years, particularly if they get more and more golfing visitors. As the resorts get popular, the prices tend to go up. But at this moment Cyprus, for instance, certainly has much to offer. I was there about eight or ten years ago when there was only one very modest golf course, the main problem the supply of water available to irrigate the course. But that has changed, I suspect because a desalination plant has been installed which is more than suitable for golf course needs. I am sure it will be only a matter of time before new eastern European countries get some part of the 'golfing bug'. Austria has already created some new courses, along with the Czech Republic, Romania, Hungary, Croatia and the like. Turkey and Cyprus are the coming places.

Offices of tourism suddenly realise that if they have a golf course with good facilities, by that I mean putting greens, a good driving range, a comfortable and easy clubhouse with decent food which isn't too expensive, and a glass of wine to complement a meal, tourism can be increased. For that you've only got to look at the southern coast of Spain. David Thomas and I opened a couple of courses there in the mid-1960s when there were less than a handful. Now it must be close on a hundred, all due to the increased interest in golf. In fact, the Costa del Sol is now known as the Costa del Golf!

The coming of the euro has made travelling a lot easier, so if you are contemplating taking a group of four, eight, twelve or whatever number, you simply need someone to organise the tickets, to find a reputable travel agent and away you go. A good investment for a travelling golfer is one of those large golf bag covers (which are not too expensive), into which you can put your golf bag, shoes, balls. It will look after your clubs while they are moved around in the belly of the aeroplane, or perhaps even thrown about when frustrated baggage handlers realise the amount of overtime they're doing will not show up in their pay packet! A lightweight suit of waterproofs, a sturdy umbrella, a few extra bits and pieces – a couple of spare gloves, if indeed you wear them, also a dozen or two good second-hand golf balls. In some foreign countries golf balls are even more expensive than they are in the UK, so be prepared.

The continent offers up all sorts of opportunities for golfers. Some people insist on going somewhere where the sun is almost guaranteed to shine. Sadly it doesn't always do that; but remember there are masses of golf courses in Sweden (although that can be expensive), Norway and also Denmark, which is one of the hidden gems of European golf. France, Germany, Portugal, northern Spain, Italy all have a great variety of courses, some tucked away and less well known than others, but offering very good value for money and a great amount of enjoyment.

But remember you may not always be able to get on the course of your desire, for a variety of reasons – there may be a club competition, the course may be closed for remedial work, you may have to play with a member, or at least be signed in by someone who is. This doesn't signify the club has lofty ambitions, it is just the way they run their affairs. So, if you're planning ahead, it's not a bad thing to check – the internet has made this easier – on which days visitors are accepted, whether they have catering arrangements, handicap limits, etc. Remember, once you have a handicap and become a travelling golfer, always take that identification with you. With so many new destinations being opened up, it's possible to fly from quite a large number of UK bases to large cities in Europe which put you within easy striking distance of your golf. If a long-haul trip takes your fancy, then America, South Africa, Australia and Asia all offer wonderful experiences, but the most amazing of all may be the advent of the Middle East with all the new courses in the deserts of Dubai.

Golf has really taken off in the Middle East, in Dubai in particular where the authorities are building up their leisure industries as a buffer against the oil running out at some future date. Huge desalination plants provide the water to keep the courses alive. It shows how golf courses can be artificially created and that it is not necessarily environmentally un-friendly, something we need to be aware of these days. The Royal and Ancient, who look after the game around the world outside America and Mexico, are working hard to spread the message of sustainable course maintenance, cutting back massively on the amounts of fertilisers and water used on the courses and taking a more naturalistic approach. Golf clubs are also working more closely with the environment agencies, such as English Nature, and preserving sites of special interest so they can be enjoyed by golfers and non-golfers alike.

But, with the cost of flying set to rise and people worrying about their carbon footprint, what of golf in the UK? Again, people usually search for the sunshine but I'm always amazed when I travel round, how many very pleasant unheralded golf courses there are in England, Ireland, Scotland and Wales, where the majority of golfers will get a lot more enjoyment than battling away on one of the better-known golf courses from the back tees with the wind blowing and the rain in their faces, having paid in excess of £100 for the privilege – that's not really the way it should be! Remember my conversation with Lee Trevino when he and I went out to play a few holes years ago? 'You and I have spent enough time playing from the back tees, let's move up here where we can enjoy it and reach all the par-fours easily in two.' Wise words!

Some people think I've played every golf course in the UK – far, far from it. Years ago most golf tournaments were played at the same course or in the same area year after year. In the earliest days of my golfing life the start of the season was usually around the Watford/Rickmansworth area where the Moor Park Golf Club and its renowned High Course hosted many events. Around Leeds, Moortown, Sand Moor and Moor Allerton were regular golfing venues and the delightful town of Harrogate with its Oakdale, Starbeck and Pannal Golf Clubs were also regular venues for professional golf. On the west coast, Royal Lytham and St Anne's near Blackpool, then down the coast to Southport with its many courses, plus Formby and Royal Liverpool at Hoylake, were all special venues. There were tournaments near Manchester at more modest clubs like Wilmslow, and of course the very handsome Mere Golf and Country Club where I won my very first proper prize money, £57 10s for finishing fourth in the *Manchester Evening Chronicle* competition! Round the corner into north Wales there was the Maesteg Golf Club at Llandudno and the North Wales Golf Club. Occasionally we played in south Wales at Ashburnham and Royal Porthcawl. A few years later St Mellion golf course was created by the Bond brothers, some ten or twelve miles north of Plymouth. It was the first Jack Nicklaus-designed course in the UK and one created on a very difficult site, a great challenge for the professionals, the Benson & Hedges Tournament being played there on many occasions. Also in the picture were Wentworth and Sunningdale on the Surrey/Berkshire borders, Walton Heath near Epsom, Little Aston in situ long before the Belfry was created just a few miles north of Birmingham, Lindrick in south Yorkshire and the Scottish courses – Gleneagles, Blairgowrie, Royal Troon, Loch Lomond, Muirfield, Carnoustie and Turnberry. Ireland has superb courses round Dublin, Belfast and County Cork. Those, apart from the many exhibition matches played for the Lord Roberts Workshops and Forces Help Society, were the extent of my golfing travels within the UK. So you see, the number played is quite meagre when you consider there are over 2,000 courses in the United Kingdom and Ireland. Those with a long amateur career will have played many more than I.

Apart from those special courses which have brought me so much enjoyment and, occasionally I confess, a bit of pain, where would I suggest you go for a trip around the UK? I have to make it quite skeletal, there are just so many, but I shall give you a list of possibles where, unless they've changed radically, you will be assured of a warm welcome. Again it is worth doing a bit of research and there are a number of guides available, while the *Golfer's Handbook* has a full listing of all clubs, including their website addresses.

SOUTH AND SOUTH-WEST ENGLAND

We shall start our travels where I learnt my golf, at the Ferndown Golf Club some six miles north of Bournemouth (heather, pine, silver birch – wonderful), a delightful part of the country, with the sea to the south, the New Forest to the north, the beautiful county of Dorset to the west, and inland waterways and intriguing beauty to the east. Ferndown has always had a special place in my heart. It was there I learned the intricacies, the pleasure and the pain of golf. My memories include the old boys who helped me so unknowingly in those very formative years from thirteen to eighteen. Ferndown was always considered by those who thought they were good players relatively easy. It's been lengthened a little over the years, and from the very back tees with wind blowing it's a pretty good test and is always in good condition.

Another delight, and not far from my second home, is Parkstone, with views across Poole Harbour and Sandbanks (which has now become one of the most expensive areas to live in the world). My brother Alec and I were professionals there from 1957 until 1970. They were wonderful, informative years. Parkstone was considered more cosmopolitan than Ferndown, they had tradesmen members (butcher, baker, candlestick-maker) along with a few dukes, earls and knights of the realm, doctors and lawyers, all mingled in with great success. Poole Harbour, the second largest natural harbour in the world, was busy but it hadn't reached the heights of commercialism we see today. Much has changed since the Alliss boys were the joint professionals; the clubhouse has been enlarged, with good catering, so it's well worth a visit.

A few miles to the west is the Dorset Golf Club, better known as Broadstone, which when played as a par-68 is one of the great tests of golf in Europe. Winston Churchill used to play golf there in the 1930s, along with Leonard Lyle who went on to become Lord Lyle of Tate & Lyle fame. (You remember them, they're still at it, flogging sugar, although they say it's a dying market.) Over the ferry at Sandbanks, to the Isle of Purbeck and some of the most spectacular views to be seen anywhere; the course was once owned by Enid Blyton, she who wrote so many wonderful books for young people, which I am told are now politically incorrect. Poo bah, I say!

Meyrick Park and Queens Park Golf Clubs, both owned and run by the Borough of Bournemouth, are a delight, although Queens Park has been squeezed over the years by a dual carriage by-pass and housing growth, but it still contains many superb holes. Meyrick Park, on the other hand, was a smaller course but if you completed the first four holes in par you felt very pleased with yourself. The professional in my day was Ernest Whitcombe, one of the three Whitcombe brothers who were such stars in the years running up to the Second World War. My brother and I took over at Parkstone on the death of Reggie, who had won the Open championship in 1938, and Charles Whitcombe was the professional at the Crews Hill Golf Club in north London.

Several new courses have sprung up within fifteen or twenty

miles of Bournemouth centre. Just outside Ringwood, near Horton, is a romantically named course called Remedy Oak, where I have the honour of being the president. In a magnificent setting, an old deer park, it is rather private but it is possible to play if you make prior arrangements, which I can't stress too strongly.

To the east of Bournemouth is Barton-on-Sea, where the course runs right along the cliff top. Sadly there's been a lot of erosion over the years and the course has been moved back, but the views away to the Isle of Wight are, when the weather is kind, quite spectacular.

And there's Highcliffe, a wonderful little 18-hole course, perhaps on the smallest acreage of any course I know, not much more than fifty acres, but a good test. If you were off-line the shot into the very small greens from the wrong angle were pretty difficult. Some would even test the likes of Tiger Woods, and if anyone shouted 'Fore', everyone on the course threw themselves to the ground!

The old Northbourne Golf Club, just north of Poole, renamed Knighton Heath years ago, as well as the new courses just outside Wimborne, Dorset, right alongside Canford School, have wonderful practice facilities and a host of young pros ready to be of help, well worth a visit.

Moving west, Budleigh Salterton is again a splendid course running along the top of the cliffs where the air is fresh (on occasions a bit too fresh). Many new courses have opened up as we travel west, including St Mellion, as we saw, the home to the Benson & Hedges tournament for a number of years, designed by Jack Nicklaus and owned by the Bond brothers, big farmers and great characters, who between them created tremendous interest in golf in the west country. Across Cornwall to Newquay, if you don't feel like golf you can always surf! But I think surfing is for those of a certain age. Up to Trevose, for many years run by Peter Gammon, who's now passed it on to his son Nick. This has always been one of my favourites. There was at one time a sign on the first tee: 'Three hours is too long for a round of golf. Get on with it.' I can still see Mr Gammon standing at the window with his binoculars looking across the course to see if anyone was dragging their feet. He looked innocent but underneath he was quite a fireball! The fourth and fifth holes run down to the most wonderful beach – wonderful to look at but with dangerous currents. It's known as Booby's Bay, so-called long before topless bathing was all the rage.

Up the coast are two great links, St Enodoc and Royal North Devon, better known as Westward Ho!, for many years the home of the great J. H. Taylor, and then on to Somerset and Minehead Golf Club, which has all the qualities of a links course, plenty of sand dunes, almost a miniature Royal Birkdale. I served out my time in the RAF Regiment at the little village of Watchet, eight or nine miles from Minehead, although I only played there once in all the time I was there. Our CO (it was an ack-ack gunnery school) was mad keen on rugby and thought anyone who played golf was a poof! So not much opportunity for me to practise my skills there. My brother, Alec, was then the professional at the Weston-super-Mare Golf Club which wasn't too far away. They had a very good collection of golfers who made me welcome on the few occasions I got to visit my brother. It was a rare treat, they would take us to the Atlantic Hotel for a vodka and tonic and steak dinner! Bliss.

WALES

When the original bridge was built over the Severn on the M4 it made Chepstow well within easy reach and St Pierre became a pleasant venue for many big golf tournaments in the late

1970s and '80s. On to Royal Porthcawl, where my father, Percy, a true Yorkshireman, started his professional career. He'd finished his service in the First World War in the Argyll & Sutherland Highlanders, and applied for a position with the Yorkshire Cricket Club, but as a back-up he'd applied for the assistant's post at Porthcawl. The letter from Royal Porthcawl came first and that's how father got embroiled in the game of golf rather than cricket.

The Bournemouth Alliance used to play the South Wales Alliance every year home and away. It was great fun, particularly when the match was played at Royal Porthcawl. We either stayed at the Esplanade or the Sea Bank hotels, both looking right over the water. Ernest Millward, who won the English Amateur Championship in 1952 at Burnham & Berrow, used to play for Bournemouth and would give me a lift in his Alvis Speed 25 which he drove with great skill but rather quickly! The first view of the links at Porthcawl was interesting: a great forbidding stone house on the right, which I discovered was a home for retired coalminers, then the car park and a low corrugated iron roof clubhouse which had been battered by many a gale, but what a warm welcome. It's very smart these days and, again, if you decide on a base where you can strike out to, say, four or five golf clubs over the space of a week, it's an absolute delight with so much history.

There are many courses in mid-Wales waiting to be discovered by the golfing visitor but I must mention a particular course in the north of the Principality. It was at Llandudno where I won the PGA Championship in 1957. It was 1 April when my brother and I took over as joint professionals at Parkstone. I helped Alec to settle in as best I could, drove off into the wide blue yonder, only to come back five days later with the Llandudno trophy and title of PGA Champion. What a way to start a new job!

NORTH-WEST ENGLAND

Round the corner is the Wirral, dotted with courses but dominated by Hoylake (or Royal Liverpool). It was there in 1949 I played with Guy Wolstenholme; we had both just signed up for our National Service. We borrowed clubs and set off on a very hot late June evening. I went round in 67 from the back tees. Borrowed clubs, army boots and all. I confess I hardly remember it but it was engraved in Wolstenholme's mind! My only clear memory of Hoylake is the terrifying first hole, out of bounds on the right all the way up to the green, and when the wind is coming at you from about eleven o'clock at 40 mph, it's not for the faint-hearted! What a wonderful return Hoylake made to the Open rota in 2006, with both the weather and the spectacular performance of Tiger Woods.

West Lancs course is well worth a visit, but you do need to be on your very best form if you're going to enjoy this experience, and don't miss Formby Golf Club whatever you do. We now enter Southport, and the Southport and Ainsdale course. Have a look at Gumleys, one of the largest bunkers you'll see in a day's march. (They have a similar one down at Royal St George's, and I'm not sure which is the bigger; when you're young and impressionable they both look about the size of St Paul's Cathedral.) The clubhouse is perched up on a bit of high ground overlooking the course with a very fine opening longish par-three, in the style of Royal Lytham and St Anne's – there's nothing wrong with that if the hole's good enough.

Follow the railway and you come to Hillside, living in the shadow of Royal Birkdale, a fine test indeed, particularly the first few holes. A large amount of very superior sand was excavated from the course years ago, making for some alterations, which have settled now but took a long time to bed in. Although spectator movement might be more difficult, it could house the Open Championship as far as the quality of the golf course is concerned.

My first experience of Royal Birkdale was the Open Championship in 1954. Looking back I had a good chance of winning, as indeed did several others. I ended up just four strokes behind the eventual winner, Peter Thomson. Little did we know then he would win four out of the next five championships, a wonderful record.

The clubhouse at Birkdale caused great consternation when it was first opened and in fact still does. I'm not sure whether it's Art Nouveau or Art Deco but in all truth it doesn't look that interesting when compared with clubhouses like Hoylake and Royal Lytham and St Anne's, but once inside, the view is a delight; the rooms are airy and you don't notice what it looks like! When the BBC and the mighty American and other world television companies came over to survey the course for the Open in 2008 they were most concerned about the way the clubhouse looked. Some didn't want to see it, it was said. Great discussions went on as to where their studios could be put and, as they pay a huge chunk of money for the privilege, it's their right to at least ask questions! Who was it who said, 'He who pays the piper calls the tune?'

I've already mentioned Royal Lytham and St Anne's, one of my favourite courses. Everything's so neat, tidy and cosy. I suppose some people might think it's claustrophobic but I like the fact the clubhouse is only a few feet from the back of the 18th green; you can look out of the big window right up the course and from the main bar look towards the first tee, putting green, and pro shop. The sturdy red-brick buildings ooze old-world charm. I love it!

If you're getting a little weary of links golf, you could always move inland, go towards Blackburn and tucked away in the hills you'll find many a delightful course ready to welcome you, then move on up towards Lancaster and the Borders. Swing east and discover Silloth-on-Solway; if ever there was a hidden gem that surely is it. Don't be fooled by the relatively flat terrain, the fairways and the greens contain many delicate contours that constantly tease the player. Great golf and great value. It was the superb woman amateur Cecil Leitch, the only real rival to Joyce Wethered, who made the club famous. It is said that the club once fielded five Leitch sisters against the men of a Scottish golf club – and won!

I nearly forgot the Lake District. I remember one of the old boys who were so kind to me when I was growing up used to tell me about the Windermere Golf Club; it was not very long, but had wonderful views across that magical part of England.

SCOTLAND

So many courses, so much variety, such good value, the great links of the Open and unheralded gems, Scotland really is the home of golf. Up the west coast to the wonderful Turnberry, then Ayr, Royal Troon, Barassie at Kilmarnock, Western Gailes, so many places for you to park your caravan, put up your tent, find a B&B or book the bridal suite at a five-star hotel. Look around, there's something for everyone. Earlier in the book I talked about Turnberry, that magical spot, now bought up by investors from Dubai who are promising to invest in upgrading both the hotel and the courses. Royal Troon is another Open venue and a classic 'out-and-back' links so if the wind doesn't get you one way, it will the other. At Prestwick we are on hallowed turf, of course. It was here that the first Open Championship took place in 1860. It has been altered a little over the years but remains steeped in fascinating history.

Across the hills into Perthshire, one of my favourite counties: There we are spoiled with Blairgowrie, the courses at the Gleneagles Hotel, due to host the Ryder Cup in 2014, and smaller ones dotted round the fair city of Perth on the way to Forfar, and north again to Aberdeen with all they have to offer.

Or head south, over the Tay and Forth bridges, on to the relatively new southern Edinburgh bypass: out in the Lothians we find Gullane – pronounced 'Gillan' and offering three courses and views over Muirfield one way and Edinburgh the other – and a host of delightful courses before you reach the mighty Muirfield itself. Oh what a delight it was staying at the Greywalls Hotel, with its comfortable furniture, the smell of burning logs, and the view from the bedroom windows across the lawn, down the 10th hole on one of the greatest, fairest golf courses in Britain, and what wonderful food. The Honourable Company of Edinburgh Golfers is one of the great clubs and has hosted many exciting Opens on its majestic links.

Take in Dunbar, North Berwick, and Musselburgh, all steeped in golfing history. You get the feeling you could blindfold someone, give them a pin, stand them in front of a map of Scotland, just say, 'Stick it wherever you like' and they'd come up with a course that would suit even the most discerning of golfers. And don't think I've forgotten Nairn and Royal Dornoch, Kingsbarns, Tain, Brora, Skibbo Castle, Leven Links, Elie, Cruden Bay – oh so many!

St Andrews

A special word about the Home of Golf itself. Although golf may be going through a slow period, there are certainly institutions, organisations and the like which will continue to prosper, despite any form of recession. I'm thinking particularly of St Andrews and its surrounding golf courses. It's amazing when you think, no matter what the brochures tell you, the season up there (for anyone other than the most hardy) is only seven months long, although the winter can produce some calm, bright, sunny days when a couple of pullovers are sufficient to keep you warm and comfortable. In 2008 the seventh course was opened, called the Castle, which is south of the town, perched on the cliffs with the most magnificent views away to the North Sea and beyond St Andrews to the hills north of Dundee. There's golf to suit everyone at St Andrews, with the monster putting green where, in the olden days, elderly ladies, with a handbag slung over their arm, aimed to hole out from the most outrageous distances; occasionally they managed to strike it towards the hole and it disappeared, much to the chagrin of other players who thought their skills were of a much higher standard than a dear old lady on a bus trip from Montrose!

The first six courses are the Eden, Jubilee, Balgove, Strathtyrum, the New (well, it was opened in 1895), and, of course, the Old Course, on which everybody wants to play. Over 200,000 rounds a year are played on the courses – quite remarkable when you think the Old Course doesn't open on Sunday. That's the day which was laid down for the locals to walk their dogs or enjoy the ambience of open spaces and the free fresh air blowing in from the North Sea. There are one or two myths about St Andrews. Many people imagine the R&A own all the golf courses, certainly the Old Course. Not true, in fact all they own is the clubhouse and a small area around it. The rest of the land belongs to the town, the council, and is run by the Links Trust, which was set up in the early 1970s.

Running the Trust entails a great deal of responsibility. The over 200,000 rounds played each year generate huge sums of money. Those monies are used to create new golfing facilities for the tens of thousands who want to visit the old town, which is not only steeped in golf but has the third-oldest university in Britain, and a blood-stained involvement commemorated in Scottish history in the Martyrs' Monument which stands on the high ground overlooking the R&A clubhouse.

It's extraordinary to recall that less than fifty years ago many people thought St Andrews was dying. Properties were not selling. In fact, the Rusacks Hotel, alongside the 18th fairway, struggled to find a buyer at the ridiculous price of £75,000. How things change. Modest house prices now knock a hole in a million pounds. The university has enlarged and flourishes and that's not all down to one of the young royals attending class there a few years ago.

One of the greatest honours of my life was to be offered honorary membership of the Royal and Ancient Golf Club. That really was a bolt from the blue! Something I had never contemplated; never did I imagine it would happen to me, but happen it did and I feel very privileged to have joined such a small, select band of former winners of the Championship and members of the royal family. I know, I know, how on earth did I get in there?

NORTH-EAST ENGLAND

Back across the border you can discover the delights of golf within a thirty-mile radius of Newcastle. How about combining a day's racing with some golf if you've won the lottery, perhaps a night at the Gosforth Park Hotel? Further south we come to Harrogate, Pannal, Oakdale, Starbeck and, of course, around Leeds, Alwoodley, Sand Moor and Moor Allerton, my old club.

Then just outside Sheffield we find Lindrick, home of the 1957 Ryder Cup when the Yorkshire steel magnate, Sir Stuart

Goodwin, saved the day by paying all the costs of running the event. I well remember my first visit to the club when John Jacobs' mother, Vivienne, was the stewardess. It was the mid-fifties when food did not appear in great abundance; however, she brought out a platter of bacon, eggs, mushrooms, kidneys, fried bread, tomatoes, baked beans, hot brown toast, home-made marmalade, pots of tea. Oh, what joy and the start of my new shape!

John's cousin, Jack Jacobs, known as 'the Duke', was the professional, and always said he had had the most wonderful life. His golf was good but his nerve was not; he was a fine shot, a good fisherman, enjoyed a game of cards. The old toffs at the club, those embroiled in the steel industry, either huge sheets of metal or the finest silver, welcomed him into their society, but Jack always 'knew his place'. A little golf, a dish of smoked salmon, a glass of champagne. Ah, yes, you see the life of a club professional can be okay! Did we miss Ganton, near Scarborough, surely not? It is one of the best inland courses in the country, although it feels as if the sea cannot be far away. Indeed, the wind plays a huge factor on this classic moorland course, with fairways bordered by gorse and heather; on a windy day it is a terrific test, on a calm one still a good challenge.

MIDLANDS

Another inland course I would put in the same category as Ganton is Woodhall Spa in Lincolnshire. A little out of the way but well worth the effort to get there. The English Golf Union now has its headquarters there and there is a second course, but the original layout is a prime example of a heathland course and the bunkering makes it a sublime test. On to Sherwood Forest and the Notts Golf Club (better known as Hollingwell), both magical places. Then over towards Birmingham and Little Aston where I won my first major tournament in 1954 – the Daks. What memories, £400 first prize, wow! Charlie Ward was the professional, one of Britain's top players just after the war.

Moving east towards Norfolk we come upon King's Lynn where David Thomas and I had the pleasure of designing one of our first courses. That was many years ago. The club has developed into a very pleasant spot to while away a few hours. Brancaster, or Royal West Norfolk, is a wonderful old links, slightly in danger of sea erosion, but a beautiful spot on a summer's day. In the wind of a winter's day it can still be a monster but if the sea is in, driving over the marsh at the 8th and the 9th is a great sight – the clubhouse can even get cut off at high tide, so check the time listed by the entrance. Hunstanton is another fine links, which has hosted many top events. Sheringham sits on downland on the cliffs above the town. It was here that Joyce Wethered, after holing a tricky putt, despite a noisy passing train, was congratulated on her concentration, replied, 'What train?'

SOUTH-EAST ENGLAND

Down the M1 to Junction 13, let's pop into Woburn to sample the delights of the little town and a possible game on one of the three courses within the Duke of Bedford's estate. Nearer to London we come to South Herts, the home of Harry Vardon and Dai Rees, a veritable oasis almost completely surrounded by housing but still managing to keep its charm and warm welcome.

Moving west we come to Huntercombe. I love the story about Lord Nuffield, the great motoring entrepreneur, who bought the course because they refused him membership. Good God, he was in trade, just a motor mechanic! Stoke

Poges, now called Stoke Park, just outside Slough, is developing into one of the finest courses north of the River Thames. It was used as a setting for Ian Fleming's *Goldfinger*, another adventure for our hero James Bond. I'll never forget how Sean Connery managed to get one over on Odd Job. What a man! *Bridget Jones's Diary* was also filmed there. What a place!

Wentworth has become familiar via the two tournaments each year that were televised, the PGA Championship in May and the World Match Play in the autumn. Sadly the World Match Play has ended, but the PGA Championship continues on the West course; however the East and the Edinburgh offer equally good golf. The East was opened at the same time as the West and was also designed by Harry Colt. It's another glorious layout but more manageable if you don't hit it as far as the modern professionals – and who does? What an area for golf around this corner of Surrey and Berkshire! There is Worplesdon, West Hill, Woking, the Berkshire, all splendid but some too 'grand' for new golfers. Maybe they are, but if you look around you'll see others in the vicinity able to cater for your needs and, you know, it's odds on Monday to Friday they will welcome you with open arms. But Tuesdays, ah, Tuesday is Ladies' Day! Swinley Forest is a very special gem, as is New Zealand, just outside Woking.

Out of London, down the M2 and the A2 towards Thanet, and you find Chestfield, a neat course, wounded by an unnecessary bypass, but a delightful clubhouse and staff that make you feel most welcome. I highly recommend it. Royal St George's and Princes, at Sandwich, and Royal Cinque Ports at Deal form a string of magnificent links courses on the coast, all Open venues but so accessible from London. A number of other clubs, less heralded, but there to be enjoyed by many, populate east Kent, such as Canterbury, another Harry Colt classic. Then there is the new Nick Faldo layout at Chart Hills.

As we go westwards, don't pass Sleaford or Brighton and Hove, perched high up on the hills – what views! Pulborough, in West Sussex, is a very pretty course with one of the great carvery luncheons of all time. Liphook, Hindhead, Farnham, Hankley Common, Old Thorns, North Hants are all to be enjoyed, as well as new courses not far from the centre of Fareham. Stoneham, just north of Southampton, is well worth a visit, although on a hot day the uphill 18th is a bit of a test!

Suddenly we're back on the edge of the New Forest heading towards Brockenhurst, Lyndhurst and other pleasant watering holes in wonderful surroundings.

There you have the whistle-stop tour, just a personal selection, and we hardly touched central England, mid-Wales and north-west Scotland – but, hey, you must visit Durness, a nine-hole course way up north, as far as you can go before you hit the Pentland Firth and the Orkneys, perched on cliffs with magnificent views; make sure it's a nice day!

Most of all, check up with the clubs before you go – and have fun!

13

REGISTERING SPECIAL INTEREST

'And now here's Jack Lemmon, about to hit that all-important eighth shot.'
JIM MACKAY, on Lemmon playing the 14th hole at Pebble Beach, *Bing Crosby National Pro-Am*, ABC-TV, 1959

Ah, the game of golf, how I love you! Although it has given me some unhappy moments, it has been absolutely magnificent, affording me the opportunity of travelling, meeting so many people. Looking back I didn't do as well as I should. If I'd tried harder and concentrated more, gone out and practised instead of sitting under a tree engaged in conversation with friends, enjoying a modest glass of wine ... But it was a great journey. I was very fortunate at the two main clubs where I was the professional – Parkstone in Bournemouth and Moor Allerton in Yorkshire – lots of time for competition play, wonderful people, what wonderful memories.

And then came a second career, of talking about the game

on television, witnessing many of the great moments in the game at first hand. It's been a great privilege. Not that I thought I might end up associated with such famous grumps as Sir Alan Sugar or Anne Robinson, accused of doing down younger generations. After all, it's not as if I go around pointing a finger at someone and barking, 'You're fired!' or dismissing them with a curt, 'You are the weakest link, goodbye!'

Have you noticed that journalists, when composing pieces about other humans, whether they be interesting, law-abiding or not, have a fetish for always telling you how old they are, and it doesn't seem to matter whether they're in their twenties, thirties, forties, or have free travel passes and are now almost ready for the knacker's yard?

Whenever my exploits are reported, somewhere in the first couple of lines we'll see the number '77', and somehow it always seems to be in bold print. You would have thought that at the age of seventy-seven most things would have passed me by and it would be almost impossible to cause any sort of ripple, particularly when engaged in commentating on the wonderful pedestrian, exciting, occasionally boring, game of golf! But I certainly managed to cause ripples, if not quite large waves, when working for BBC TV at the PGA Championship, played on Wentworth's West Course in May 2008. There had already been quite a few articles in magazines and newspapers alerting us to the fact that several of the top British and Irish players would not be on view because they didn't feel the golf course suited their style of play; nevertheless the field was first-class, the prize fund huge and the weather reasonably good but there were a couple of drawbacks for our golfing gladiators.

Over the last thirty or forty years the game of golf has been basically played through the air. Now, don't laugh! By that I mean a great number of players are now six foot tall and more, have thirty-four-inch waists, and arms that would do credit to a blacksmith. The modern technique, with a deep-faced driver, is to tee it high and let it fly – launch the ball as quickly as you can, zoom it into the sky, aiming at beautifully prepared fairways, which are watered just enough to give the ball a little cushion. From there another high shot, plummeting down on to the greensward before, hopefully, nestling by the flag, from where the game of putting takes over.

But it wasn't quite like that this year at Wentworth. There was a stiff wind blowing, and because the course is tree-lined on all but a few holes, which run in every direction, it's never easy to judge which direction the wind is coming from, which makes club selection difficult, painful and often tedious. How often have we seen players, after much deliberation with their faithful caddies, having pored over their copious notes for what seems like an eternity, come up short or go too far. Then there's the look of anguish on the face, the arms thrown up in horror, wondering how on earth they could be twenty yards out one way or t'other. Getting round a course when these conditions prevail takes a very different technique, which a far greater number of players were able to do in times long ago before fairway watering became the norm.

It all began rather gently on that breezy Thursday morning, but it was a drying wind and in the space of thirty-six hours the fairways became fast and running, the greens started to seed. Not that the rank and file of club golfers would have noticed any difference, but to some of the players involved it was like putting on greens that had been covered in lumps of coal! Well, there I was, with my fellow BBC workers, watching the play unfold on our various monitors, realising that the *crème de la crème* of the golfing world were struggling. Indeed, I made the comment that years ago, before thousands of gallons of water were poured on to the sixty or seventy acres of prepared grass, players learned different techniques. You had to keep the ball lower, pick out a spot maybe twenty or thirty yards short of the green, using the contours as best you could, to get the ball near the hole. There was not the luxury of getting your yardage right and then lobbing the ball right to the target and watch it spin about like a herring on a gridolo. The game was more cunning or difficult, you had to use different techniques to get round the course successfully.

I quoted a few names who had mastered that technique, Peter Thomson, Ken Bousfield, Bernard Hunt, Christy O'Connor and, dare I say it, myself. Neil Coles was the master of Wentworth, indeed he was known as the West Course specialist. His caddie for many years, Chingy Maidment, told anyone who would listen it was because he was able to keep the ball below the level of the treetops; this way, for most of the time, there was very little deviation of ball flight. To be successful you had to play this type of golf when hard bouncy conditions prevailed.

Years ago there were many classic examples of these skills – Peter Thomson winning the *Yorkshire Evening News* tournament at the Sand Moor golf course on the northern outskirts of Leeds, when the fairways were the colour of brown bread and the greens, which were rather small, sticking out in as bold a green as you've ever seen. In those days greens were watered by hand, a standpipe beside each green to which a hosepipe was connected and there a noble green-keeper would stand, directing water on to the prepared surface. He alone decided when he thought there was sufficient water, and then he'd move on to the next hole. Thomson was absolutely supreme. I don't know what club he took off most of the tees, but I suspect a three-wood to keep the ball in play. He then managed to hit the small targets every time with a short-iron and when he didn't like the idea of trying to pitch on the green, landed the ball short and let it run forward towards the target. A difficult thing to do, particularly on a course with lots of little rolls and humps and slopes, so there was much to think about. It wasn't quite as simple as the game played today.

My words were taken slightly out of context (well, that's happened many a time) and it just so happened there was a players' meeting going on at Wentworth at that time and allegedly the question of my criticism was brought up. Nick Dougherty said he thought my remarks were disgusting. (He actually said 'disgusting'.)

Now, I take some of this with a pinch of salt because I know journalists are able to phrase questions that catch out the unwary, and, on occasions, some of the very wary. On the last day of the event, a message came through that John Hopkins of *The Times* and a gentleman from the *Daily Mirror* named Neil McLeman wondered if they could come and have a talk. We agreed a time and they came to the studio, where I was sitting in our little rest area with Gary Lineker and John Shrewsbury, who, for many years, produced golf and other sports for the BBC. I asked them to remain, as I thought it might not be a bad idea to have a couple of witnesses just in case things blew out of all proportion.

The gentlemen of the press wanted to know what I thought of being 'ripped' by young Dougherty and did I think I had anything to answer for? In fact they gave the impression that player power was on the move and there might even be a movement to oust the seventy-seven-year-old Alliss from his position within the BBC. Allegedly, Dougherty, when asked by a member of the press whether he agreed with me that they weren't playing very well, had remarked, 'I'd like to take him out there and show him how difficult it is!'

Now that remark rather incensed me. Having won twenty-one tournaments in a period of fifteen years, competed in ten World Cups and played in eight Ryder Cups, if there was anybody on this planet who knew how difficult conditions on a golf course could be, it was me. I banged the table and said just that.

We talked a little bit more and off they went, and I wondered whether they would report what they'd been told fairly and accurately. The next day I bought several newspapers, slightly in fear and trepidation as to whether or not I would be portrayed as an ageing idiot who had no idea about the modern game of golf. In fact I had to buy newspapers for another few days to get all the responses from the various golfing journalists, and I'm pleased to say that 99 per cent of them were favourable. I did not expect any favours however from Lawrence Donegan of the *Guardian*. Over the years Mr Donegan has had several digs at me and he does have a sharp turn of phrase. He wrote:

In Peter Alliss no caricature is too extreme, no insult too, well, insulting when it comes to the BBC's Voice of Golf. Being a hip young thing I have done more than my share of caricaturing and insulting through the years, and looking back I stand by every word. Alliss is, after all, truly awful. As a golf commentator he is self-absorbed, in love with the sound of his own voice almost as much as he is out of touch with what's going on in golf circa 2008. Furthermore his social and political opinions were formed in the acidic surroundings of the 1950s gentlemen's room and don't appear to have changed since. Not a crime in itself, of course, except that he occasionally foists these opinions on the rest of us while we are trying to watch Monty missing another putt. He should shut up. This rant, with its plaintive yearning for the good old days, would normally serve as further evidence of Alliss' failings but for the rather inconvenient fact that the BBC's man was absolutely right.

So, in the space of a few sentences of set insults he came round to my side. But he, along with a few others who wrote more kindly, seemed to miss the main drift of my argument. After all, it could be argued that modern golfers have no reason to learn to play 'a different game' because they never meet those conditions, and perhaps we were lucky to have experienced more of the vagaries of the game of golf.

Look at every other walk of life. If you took five top Formula 1 racing drivers and, without any tuition, introduced them to five motorcars made in 1903, telling them to start them up and drive to Brighton, how many do you think would be able to turn the engine over, let alone drive out of the car park – those who had never experienced a crash gearbox or cranked a car up by hand?

Footballers complain about pitches that have a bumpy surface, yet many people of mature years remember the days, before colour television came in, of watching, say, Wolverhampton Wanderers playing Honved on a pitch where you could almost count the blades of grass, with the game played through a sea of two-inch mud with a heavy solid leather ball and players running about with footwear that was only just a whisker lighter than army boots.

Not so long ago, Wimbledon's grass seemed to wear out more quickly and if you get the opportunity to pick up and handle one of those wooden tennis rackets, which were the only ones available, you wonder how they managed to be so skilful.

How do you think the top dozen golfers in the world would do if you took them to one of our championship courses on a windy day and gave them the clubs and balls that were available a hundred years ago? How many would break 85, and yet if you look at the record book, you'll find the players of the day were going round St Andrews, Prestwick, Carnoustie and the like in the mid-70s. This was long before the coming of the cylindrical lawnmower or gang mowers and tractor to cut the fairways. Back then a handful of sheep and a green-keeper with a razor-sharp scythe kept the grass cut. The courses were shorter by 500 or 600 yards, but the bunkers weren't raked and until Gene Sarazen invented the sand iron, getting out of bunkers was a cross between a work of art, in some cases great strength, and very precise striking, with the most lofted club in the bag, with a knife-like leading edge.

So you see, what I was really talking about was modern players never having had the experience of how to negotiate their way more successfully round a hard, fast-running, windy course, and, you could argue, why should they? But looking back, I thank the Lord for all those exhibition matches I played for the Lord Roberts' Workshops and Forces Help Society, along with Bernard Hunt, Dai Rees and David Thomas. Off we went sixteen to eighteen times a year, playing on golf courses the length and breadth of the country, up on the hills, down in the dales, heathland, hard-baked clay, playing in front of three or four hundred and, if we were very lucky, at a big venue six or seven hundred spectators who had all paid two shillings (10p) to come and watch our efforts. Oh, what great fun it was, and how much we learnt about the game of golf from those happy informative days.

A young player approached me earlier in the year and said he'd played at my old club at Parkstone and wondered how I'd got a reputation for being such a good long-iron player, as basically the golf course was short. The longest club he played for his second shot was a three-iron, and that at the par-fives 11th and 17th. I told him that I found Parkstone, and indeed Ferndown, where I really learnt my early golf, both ideal clubs to learn about long play. He stared at me with an amazed look on his face, 'How did you do it then?' I said, 'Well, it's very simple. Can you remember the first hole at Parkstone (about 380/390 yards)?' 'Yes, very well.' 'Well, instead of taking a driver off the tee, why not hit a five-iron, or indeed an eight-iron, then you're left with a four-wood to the green, and so on and so on?' He gave me a look that made me feel somewhere between a golfing messiah and someone capable of winning every session of *Mastermind* and *Who Wants to Be a Millionaire?*

It's so simple if you use your brain, if you explore various possibilities. That's one of the good things about leaving school when you're fourteen; if you're lucky enough you meet interesting people and by the time you're twenty-one it's amazing how much knowledge you will have gleaned if you've paid attention.

14

THE PRESS TENT

'You can't trust anybody these days.'
TV commentator PETER ALLISS on witnessing American Walker Cup golfer Doug Clarke bless himself before attempting a bunker shot – and leaving the ball in the sand.

How techniques have changed and how lucky I have been! It's amazing really but I've met or played golf with at least 75 per cent of the players who have won our Open Championship over the last hundred years. Some of my father's contemporaries and golfing friends were players who had won the Open – Alf Padgham, Alf Perry, Dick Burton, Fred Daly, Henry Cotton, Reggie Whitcombe – in fact looking back and remembering those times, I can almost pinpoint the first time I ever saw, heard and virtually felt a golf ball being 'hit' in a way that was different from anything I'd ever seen or heard before, that great 'crack' when clubhead hit ball, and the various styles. Alf Padgham, the Open Champion in 1936, had a slow, languid swing, whereas Reg Whitcombe was quick and aggressive. Alf Perry was rather agricultural, Burton had a flail at the top of the back swing, Cotton began his back swing hands first, à la Bobby Jones.

At that time most of the golfing world played the game with a ball measuring 1.62 inches. The Americans in the early 1920s had experimented with and produced a ball measuring 1.68 inches. This was due to a number of reasons. Firstly, in many states they had a much coarser grass which grew thicker, therefore they wanted a ball that sat up a little bit more. On the other hand, being keen businessmen, they didn't see why they should buy all the moulds and various items of golf ball manufacturing equipment from Britain. So, they changed the dimensions, and their own vast business empire began.

Looking back at the equipment players used in the 1930s and '40s, it's hard to visualise what very good ball-strikers they were. For driving, the ball was invariably teed low, the clubheads were made of wood and much experimentation was done to find a substitute for persimmon, a wood found mostly in Florida. Oak, beech, elm were tried and all found wanting. The wood itself was either too heavy or split easily, so persimmon it was. But during the war years golf was a frivolity and persimmon was not harvested for that purpose, so at the end of hostilities there was very little seasoned stock left. That quickly ran out, so club manufacturers were faced with using green wood which was not up to the task. Inserts were introduced, made of either ivory or some sort of fibre, to cushion the clubhead against damage. Compared to today's equipment it looked rather crude.

An interesting fact – the grips at that time were basically all leather or chamois, and were taken quite a long way down the shaft. I never discovered the reason for this. The iron faces were not lined, they were punched, which when done by hand, producing slightly uneven indentations which could grip and hold the ball very successfully, but in later years this was deemed illegal.

Golf was always played with the hands and a good stance was always important but with the coming of steel shafts, the hands played an even bigger role in the making of good players. This was accentuated by Henry Cotton who, when teaching, used to get his pupils to whack a heavy car tyre so as to get used to the idea of applying right hand and clubhead to the ball. Although I haven't seen it used today, it's a very good and simple tactic for strengthening your hands without actually having to go to the practice ground. So if you have an old tyre and a bit of room, lay it out, get an iron and whack away. You'll be amazed how soon you start to strengthen your wrists, but use an old iron as if used a lot the shaft will bend and may even break.

> *'How are you getting on with your new clubs?' asked the golfer when he walked into the bar and saw a friend of his. 'Fine,' replied the friend. 'They put twenty yards on my slice.'*
> DAI REES, *Dai Rees on Golf*, 1959

Like early equipment, the condition of the early courses by today's standards was poor, although at the time we thought they were magnificent. How well I remember my first trips to the fabled golf courses where the Open Championship was played! Royal Liverpool (or Hoylake as it's more popularly known), St Andrews, Carnoustie. Although by today's standards the greens would have been considered slow, to me they were superb.

The war ended in 1945 but it really wasn't until the early fifties that things began to get back to normal. The manufacture of golf clubs had restarted and golf ball manufacturers were back in business, but there was still room for those other companies who re-covered second-hand golf balls. It was fun to go out on the course, search around, find umpteen balls, then pack them off to a company in Birmingham called Golf Ball Developments Ltd, who produced a top-quality ball called a Penfold, and their cheaper version known as a Bromford. What actually happened to old balls was this, the cover was removed and a new one vulcanised on. The attraction was you could have whatever name you wished stamped on the ball – sometimes it was the professional's name or that of the golf club, which just added a personal touch. They sold for about two bob (10p) each.

Oh, how I enjoyed playing through the fifties and sixties, they were my grand years.

I enjoyed the players of the day. I especially enjoyed Max Faulkner, delightfully eccentric, one of the finest strikers of the ball I've ever seen, who played magical golf with the most ill-assorted clubs you ever saw in your life. Gus, his father, bought the then derelict Selsey Golf Club just after the war, so his son could have somewhere to practise and prepare for winning the Open Championship, which he did in 1951. Max boasted he hit a thousand practice balls every day and milked twenty cows to strengthen his wrists! He drank the strongest tea of any person I've met in my life. When tea bags first came in he'd have five or six stuffed in a mug, and the spoon virtually stood straight up in it. What it did to his insides I have no idea but it certainly discoloured the drinking mug!

Then came the players from overseas just after the war. The first two invaders were Australian Norman von Nida and South African Bobby Locke, and between them they pretty much dominated the European scene until well into the early fifties. Then along came Peter Thomson, who won the Open Championship in 1954, '55 and '56. He missed out in '57, giving Bobby Locke victory, but won again in 1958 in a playoff with David Thomas, so he was within a whisker of winning five in a row.

There was also another South African, Gary Player, who won the Open in 1959 at Muirfield and dozens more events big and small. John Jacobs and I watched him practising impossible pitch shots from a downhill lie on to a sloping green that was just baked clay, the place Crans-sur-Sierre in Switzerland, the year 1955. He asked us what we thought of his game; we suggested he should go back to South Africa and get a club job. We said it in the nicest possible way. I'm sure he's glad he didn't take that advice!

In 1960 Arnold Palmer arrived. What a hullabaloo, what excitement! We hadn't seen anything like this since the days of Walter Hagen – crash, bang, wallop, what a picture! What a photograph! It was in the days when smoking was fashionable; he devoured at least twenty cigarettes a round, hitched up his trousers, looked everybody straight in the eye and thundered his way round the golf course in amazing fashion.

Then lo and behold, Jack Nicklaus turned professional and swept into the arena. At the time he had a crew-cut hairdo, was overweight and had an ugly swing, but he was seeing off all his challengers in the most remarkable fashion. It's rather forgotten now but Billy Casper dominated the game if you took the big three, Player, Palmer and Nicklaus, out of the equation. He was majestic and never got the credit he deserved. Johnny Miller was the brightest of stars but only for a few years in the mid-seventies.

As for Doug Sanders, did you ever see such a funny little swing, but such a marvellous competitor? He, too, disappeared in the mists of time. Why? Probably because he three-putted the last green at St Andrews to let Jack Nicklaus win the championship in 1970, when victory may have changed many things, but it wasn't to be.

The home players were greatly encouraged every year by the press and public, and although one or two got close, no victory came their way. The wonderful Christy O'Connor,

Bernard Hunt, Neil Coles, all came close in the sixties, so many different styles and personalities, which all go to make up this amazing game.

Many people were saying Arnold Palmer 'saved' our Open. He certainly brought a new wave of interest and, in turn, encouraged other great players from the United States to come and play, which they did: Lee Trevino, one of the greatest of all time, Ray Floyd, Hale Irwin, Tom Watson, Craig Stadler and many more. Golf was to become huge business; you only had to go into a good professional's shop to see how many items were on sale.

There have been a number of great moments which shouldn't be forgotten, but everything has rather paled into insignificance since the coming of Tiger Woods. He has shown over the last twelve years (yes, it really is that long) his prowess in playing the game at the highest level. So consistent. A remarkable talent. As an amateur he won everything there was to win in the United States, then turned professional and carried on in similar vein, setting all sorts of records which may never be beaten. But then we said that about Jack Nicklaus's eighteen majors, which Tiger is chasing. Mind you, he's still got to win four more, so he's got a lot of work to put in if he's going to beat that incredible record.

Great players all have a special aura about them. Some appear to be rather shy, even self-effacing, but you don't get to the top of the tree unless you have some inner qualities which don't always show. This was certainly the case with Peter Thomson and Bobby Locke, embellished by Nicklaus and Palmer; Lee Trevino was a little noisy, even bordering on being cocky, but he did it all with a smile; Seve Ballesteros was a genius; and a number of other continental players like Jose Maria Olazabal played super golf; Sandy Lyle and Ian Woosnam – none of them in any way created an unpleasant aura around them and yet many of them, not all, seemed to float above the heads of the others as if on another planet. That's certainly true of Tiger Woods, who is so far ahead of the rest it's almost embarrassing,

Of course, there will come a time when Tiger Woods finally fades from view. We saw it with Johnny Miller, Tony Jacklin and several others. It's not just a question of diminishing skills, the nerves go, and once they've gone you might just as well pack it in and find an honest trade! Seve Ballesteros is a classic example of someone with enormous talent whose nerves have sadly affected him. He was one of the most joyous players it's ever been my privilege to watch. And what a sportsman.

Mind you, a few of the great players could sometimes irritate their opponents. They could upset or put off anyone who might be watching for those particular moments. You want to know what sort of thing they got up to? Well, when it's your turn to putt, they just happen to be in your eye-line, just on the very edge of it, not taking a bit of notice of what you're doing, just practising their putting stroke. Now, was this an accident or were they being inconsiderate, were they doing it on purpose? If you were teed up near the box and your opponent is wearing white shoes, he would move just as you were about to hit, taking a step so you'd see those white shoes move; an old trick and it's been done on many occasions! Rattling coins in the pocket, tearing the velcro on the back of a glove at an inappropriate moment, 'accidentally' standing on your line and generally being a bit of a pain; knocking down spike marks, repairing something on the green without asking your partner/opponent/companion (call them what you like). All these little moves are subtle and are done by a small percentage of the players. But, as a friend of mine in the insurance business says, '10 per cent of the drivers have 90 per cent of the accidents.'

We haven't mention Nick Faldo! I saw him play in the early 1970s; he had a rather long, flailing, willowy swing which suited his slim body. He met up with a professional named David Ledbetter and together they set out to transform his swing and, by God, they did. Faldo put on a couple of stones in weight and suddenly looked like the stand-in for Harrison Ford, and went on to win six majors, although I felt somehow his flamboyance had gone. When he was a flailer and wonderful putter, 63s and 64s flowed from his clubs, but suddenly a really cracking round was 67, but a bad one was never worse than 72.

The Hale Irwins of this world are very few and far between. His longevity, enjoying a highly lucrative pension on the Senior Tour, is remarkable. Tom Watson was brisk in all he did – the walk, the strike and, for a period, the most wonderful holer-out from ten feet. But suddenly the putter started to betray him and Tom was too proud (rather like Hogan), to ever attempt to put the ball into the hole by other devious methods – long putters, short putters, one-handed, left-handed, back-handed, cack-handed – none of that for him. Whereas Sam Snead, who would be one of my selections for the top hundred sportsmen or women of all time, would try anything to get the ball in the hole – croquet, side-saddle, you name it – Sam tried it and was successful!

No matter how much you try to hold back time, there comes a moment when the skills start to diminish. Some people choose to retire early while still at the top of their game, but usually they hang on a little bit too long. This could be for a variety of reasons – if you're into your forties and had a good season, you are expected to be there the following year to fulfil obligations which popped up during the previous season. So it's not always easy to retire.

Looking at things realistically, and I hope not too gloomily, the likes of Ernie Els, Retief Goosen, Colin Montgomerie, and even Tiger Woods, could be getting close to the moment when they say, 'Enough, do I call it a day or soldier on?'

There's no doubt over the past few seasons both Goosen and Els have gone off the boil. This intrigues me because both have made alterations to their swings. Why they would do that is something which has baffled me. As far as Colin Montgomerie is concerned, much as I would like it to happen, I don't think there's going to be a glorious autumnal finish to Colin's career.

Two early lady professionals who I had the good fortune to play with on a number of occasions were Jean Donald and Jessie Anderson, both Scottish and both delightful companions. Jessie signed up with the Dunlop Sports Company and Jean took her talents to Slazengers. There were no tournaments when they turned pro but they went round the country promoting their company's wares, playing in exhibition matches, and generally spreading the golfing gospel, which they did very well.

I was fortunate enough to play with Jean Donald in the Sunningdale Foursomes, winning on two occasions, the second time when she played under her married name of Jean Anderson. They were very happy times, although for the ladies they were blighted by the lack of opportunity to compete and show off their skills. This also applied to Wanda Morgan, a charming lady, also a very good player, but there were so few tournaments for them. How different it's been over the last thirty years or so.

Over in America the game was producing many very promising amateurs who quickly signed professional forms when they saw there was a good living to be made playing the game professionally. The Ladies Professional Golf Association was formed and what a start they had with the likes of Patty Berg, Babe Zaharias and Louise Suggs. Then came some magical names – Barbara Romack, Mickey Wright, Marlene Stewart, Jo Anne Gunderson, Nancy Lopez, Beth Daniel, Juli Inkster – the list went on and on. Perhaps the most remarkable was a young French woman called Catherine Lacoste, an amateur, who went to play in the 1967 US Women's Open Championship and, would you believe it, won it. An amateur from France winning the Open Championship? Unbelievable! She went back to France and into the the family business – you know Lacoste, the crocodile motif, one of the most recognisable sporting goods companies in the world. She got married and had a child and then, two years later, perhaps on a whim, decided to go back to the United States, this time to play in the Amateur Championship and, dammit, won again! Remarkable.

Hollis Stacey, Jan Stephenson from Australia, Sandra Haynie and, coming right up to date, Annika Sorenstam and Karrie Webb enjoyed great success and there can be no forgetting our own Laura Davies, who won the US Open in 1987. The emergence of Asian golfers has been quite staggering over the last fifteen or twenty years, with Se Ri Pak acting as a pioneer when she won two major championships as a rookie in 1998. Although there have been several home-grown Americans who have delighted the very partisan galleries, as we look at today's fields they are dominated by Lorena Ochoa, the young woman from Mexico. She who made quite a slow start to her professional career, rather like Tom Watson, and got an early reputation of being too nervous to finish the job. But once she had mastered that facet of the game, she practically won every week. When she came to Britain to play in our Women's Open at St Andrews in 2007 she won in fine style.

What a lot of men don't realise is they could learn a lot more by following, watching and absorbing the technique used by women rather than trying to emulate John Daly or Tiger Woods! Rhythm, balance, timing all come into play for women, who have less physical strength.

As the first president of the professional women's circuit in Europe when it came into being three decades ago, I've never really understood why women's golf hasn't taken off in a huge way in Britain and on the continent. All I know is, watching women play has been a revelation, from the wonderfully free and flamboyant Laura Davies, to the perkiness of Sorenstam, to the cuteness of Ochoa, and the smiles – yes, the smiles.

And what of the amateur game? Again I've been fortunate, watching the great players from an early age – Jimmy Bruen, Ronnie White, Phillip Scrutton, who was killed so tragically in a car smash on the straight road that goes past the old Blackbushe Airport in Hampshire. With him was a young assistant from Sunningdale, John Pritchett, a most promising young player, both of them dying instantly in a horrendous way. Others who were superb players were Joe Carr, Michael Bonallack, Frank Stranahan, Sam McCready, Richard Chapman, Reid Jack, Harvie Ward, the list goes on and on.

As a young up-and-coming player in the early days of apprenticeship at Ferndown Golf Club, I thought one of the most perfect lives would be to live in a lovely area, which Ferndown was, or Sunningdale or Formby, Southport or St Andrews, and have a settled job and be a very good golfer, able to tour the world playing in all the great amateur events. My model was Joe Carr, who had a ladies' fashion business in Dublin. How I envied him! He won our Amateur Championship a few times and those of his own country, Ireland, on many occasions. He was invited to play in the Masters, became a personal friend of the great players of the day – Palmer, Nicklaus and Player. He played them with carefree abandon for a few dollars, and I'm sure he wasn't always handing over money to them.

Some great names have come from the amateur ranks, going back some twenty-five years – José Mariá Olazabal, who beat Colin Montgomerie in the Amateur final at Formby in 1984, Peter McEvoy, winner in 1977 and '78 but beaten by

Paul Mayo in 1987 – what a turn-up for the book! Today amateur golf struggles. By that I mean the rewards offered in the professional game are so tempting that, unless you are of a special breed, you immediately turn pro if you have any amateur success.

Many women have turned professional in recent years, but some remain true to their roots. Linda Bayman, a tremendous character and great player, went on to captain all sorts of amateur teams and fly the flag for Britain. Alison Nicholas, on the other hand, enjoyed a fine professional career, joining Laura Davies in 1987 by winning the US Women's Open quite magnificently. In 2009 she becomes the European Solheim Cup captain in the women's version of the Ryder Cup.

Just as watching the best players on television is a way of absorbing yourself in this great game of golf, so is reading about the game. There is a great golfing literature to enjoy and nothing provides a better stimulus, perhaps in the dead of winter when you have been kept off the course by atrocious weather. I've heard it said that the smaller the ball, the better the writing about a game. Certainly, there is fine writing on golf and cricket, and, in America, on baseball. But does that mean there is no quality writing to be found on football or rugby? I'm not sure that's true, and what about sports that don't have balls at all? Strangely, some of the finest sports writing and autobiographical books have been written about the brutal world of boxing, that hardest of all pastimes, games, occupations, call it what you will. Golf isn't like that, although the mental strain can be great and has got to many over the years. But certainly in golf there are some fine books to be found and the game has always attracted writers in the newspapers with a true passion for golf.

The way sport is now reported is quite different from in my youth. You could say they were much more innocent times. Scandals, as such, were thin on the ground, people got married and one's private life was, to a large extent, kept private, but certainly in golf, with the coming of Desmond Hackett of the *Daily Express*, Jack Wood of the *News of the World*, and Ron Heager (also of the *Express* group), things began to change.

Prior to that, the major writers on the game of golf were Bernard Darwin, who wrote copious articles and newspaper pieces about the glories of the game, a sort of serious P. G. Wodehouse, Peter Ryde of *The Times*, Henry Longhurst of *The Sunday Times* and Pat Ward-Thomas of *Guardian* fame. There were other excellent writers – Bob Ferrier, Mark Wilson, Renton Laidlaw and a number of other journalists – but those first four, plus Leonard Crawley of the *Daily Telegraph*, were the heavy artillery. The reason? They were afforded space, they could be expansive in their writing. There was one journalist named Jack Statter, a man with a remarkably nimble mind, who wrote a golf column in the early days of *The Sun* newspaper. *The Sun* then, and indeed now, did not offer a large amount of space for reporting the game of golf. I don't know why, because I'm sure hundreds of thousands of their devoted readers would at some time spend hours out on the greensward. Peter Dobereiner wrote of Statter that he was 'a genius, of that there is no doubt. The form of his genius is difficult to define because his special talent was simply for living.'

There were many stories about Leonard Crawley, who, apart from writing about golf, was a fine sportsman, an elegant golfer, first-class shot and a magnificent cricketer, who once took a touring team to South Africa and played county cricket for Essex. He was a schoolmaster, running a delightfully eccentric school, where any boys who showed aptitude for fast or indeed any sort of bowling, were taken out of class and made to bowl at the great man for hours on end so that he could perfect his off-drives and late cuts!

He was a large man with a ruddy face and great white moustache, and insisted on wearing the most flamboyant clothes. He must have weighed sixteen stone and at times looked like Father Christmas. Once he bought a couple of exotic suits while covering a Walker Cup match in America! I remember one, a cross between deep red and maroon; it got an awful lot of outings, along with a Panama hat that had seen better days. They made him instantly recognisable.

Sometimes he got bored with what was happening and used to cut along home early. There were a couple of famous occasions when so and so (five shots ahead with three holes to go) was obviously going to win, and Crawley reported it as such, only for the leader to be disqualified or a challenger finished birdie, birdie, eagle, birdie to snatch the trophy. But even those errors didn't get him the sack.

Bernard Darwin, when reporting on Max Faulkner's victory in the 1951 Open Championship at the splendid Portrush Golf Club in Northern Ireland, was told after Faulkner's victory, 'Come quickly, Bernard, come quickly! We're meeting up with Max Faulkner, he's going to tell us how he won the championship!' (This was long before press rooms and press conferences, electronic typewriters and the like.) Darwin supposedly uttered the immortal words, 'My readers don't wish to know what Faulkner thought about winning the Open Championship, they want to know what I thought about his victory!'

On another occasion, during some important match, the players were dragging their feet (well, three hours for a round of golf in those days was a lifetime and should have warranted a good flogging), the players were dawdling, Darwin ended his piece with the wonderful words, 'At this stage so and so was two-up and it was time for tea.' End of story.

Pat Ward-Thomas was a fascinating character. He was in the

Royal Air Force during the Second World War; was shot down and imprisoned for a number of years. There were stories of him and others creating a couple of golf holes in their prison camp. I believe the Red Cross even sent a few clubs and some golf balls, so the inmates could practise their golf, but Pat had one helluva temper, almost bordering on the psychopathic. He was always losing his reading glasses and his temper would get more and more heated. On one occasion, whilst reporting the Open Championship from Royal St George's, he was in a terrible state. His 'readers' had been missing all day. Only when he went to get into his car, long after the close of play for the day, did he find them on the seat and was heard to yell at the top of his voice, 'There you are, you little shits!!' He had a wonderful turn of phrase, loved golf and, like Ryde, Longhurst and, to a lesser degree, Crawley, wrote quite beautifully and passionately about the game.

Longhurst wrote for *The Sunday Times* and never missed an edition for more than twenty years. He wrote some books (I'm pleased to have the complete set). Interesting titles – *Only on Sundays, Never on Weekdays, You Never Know Till You Get There*. If you've not come across any of his work, I urge you to go to your nearest library or second-hand bookshop and find anything by Longhurst – it will be a delightful read, full of emotional and emotive words.

The 'new boys' came in and obviously were encouraged to change the face of golf by their then sports editors. Desmond Hackett was quite outrageous but away from the hurly-burly of his job he was a delightful character. His trademark was a brown derby (a bowler hat, but coloured dark brown). He was heavily critical of a number of things. He became the main sports writer of the *Daily Express*, writing one grand full-page article a week but on occasions adding to that when something exciting was going on in the world of golf.

Ron Heager was the foot soldier out on the course,

reporting the everyday golf tournaments. Ron was a good fellow but I found him rather sneaky, rather like one or two journalists around today who come up in an obsequious way and ask seemingly innocent questions which they then manage to turn round, making you sound bitter and twisted, jealous or just a plain simple twerp.

Jack Wood, another man with a fine war record in the Royal Air Force, was a much jollier character but he worked for the *News of the World*, who demanded their pound of flesh and flamboyant tales, which Jack seemed to find in great abundance. But underneath it all was an underlying love of the game.

There aren't many journalists today who are just allowed to concentrate on the game but, on the whole, golf has been well served by those who have chronicled the game's deeds. Two of my particular favourites, now gone to the press tent in the sky, were Peter Dobereiner, of *The Guardian* and then *The Observer*, and Ian Wooldridge, of the *Daily Mail*. Wooldridge was an all-rounder, who wrote with authority on all manner of sports, and at many Olympics, but whose true loves were cricket and golf. Here are a couple of examples of their stylish and amusing style.

WALTER MITTY TAKES A CRACK AT THE OPEN

by Peter Dobereiner

Once upon a time the championship committee of the Royal and Ancient golf club of St Andrews was made up of trusting men who took the world at face value. No trace of cynicism tainted their natures. In their own circle if a chap said he was eight-handicap a chap did not have to ask the chap to produce a handicap certificate because a chap's word was a sacred bond. Dammit, if a chap couldn't trust a chap then what would the world be coming to, eh?

Thus it came about that when an entry was received for the 1965 Open Championship from Walter Danecki of Milwaukee his name went straight into the draw for the qualifying rounds. After all the chap described himself as a professional golfer on the entry form, plain as day.

Danecki's appearance at Hillside caused no comment. He looked as much like a golfer as anyone else, a strapping six-footer of some forty-three summers. However, as soon as he swung a club it became obvious that Walter had not devoted too many of those summers to perfecting the arts of the royal and ancient game. He breezed around Hillside in a cool 108, a score which aroused the curiosity of the ever-alert golfing press.

Danecki explained that in fact he was a mail sorter 'but I wanted the crock of gold so my conscience made me write down "professional"'. His golf credentials were, admittedly, meagre, consisting of seven years of occasional rounds over his local municipal course at $1.50 a time. The formalities for joining the PGA were too complicated and protracted and so he hit upon this idea of the British Open to cut through the red tape. 'What I will do is win one of the big ones and then they will have to let me in.' He added that he was self-taught, thought he could beat Arnold Palmer, and that he adhered to the spirit of the Professional Golfers' Association rules insofar as, not being a member, he did not charge for lessons.

The Royal and Ancient officials pondered the subject of Walter Danecki and came up with the statesmanlike solution which successive British governments had applied to most of the intractable problems of international affairs: ignore it and perhaps it will go away. They nominated a substitute to take Danecki's place in the second round, confident that he would lose no time in returning to Milwaukee.

Alas for their optimism, Danecki reported to the tee for his second round, eager to repair the damage of that opening

108. 'I don't like to quit. I like golf. That's what I came here to do.' He started, 7, 7, 8, and then, as the Americans say, the wheels came off and he scored 113, giving him a total which failed to qualify for the Open Championship by 75 strokes.

There is not, you might think, much that a golfer can say of a positive, heartening nature after such a performance. Walter was up to the challenge of the moment: 'I want to say that your small ball is right for this sort of course. If I had been playing our bigger ball I would have been all over the place.' All in all, he conceded, he was slightly discouraged by the events of these two days because, after all, he had been after the money.

This experience, as you may imagine, alerted the R&A. Steps were taken to ensure that such an embarrassing fiasco could never happen again. Really? Eleven years later another entry from a professional escaped the scrutiny of the committee. Maurice Flitcroft, a 46-year-old crane driver from Barrow-in-Furness, had set his heart on winning the old claret jug and the fortune and glory which went with it. His apprenticeship for the qualifying ordeal was even sketchier than Danecki's for his association with the game was both brief and nominal. He had taken up golf 18 months previously and his experience was limited to hitting shots on the beach. When he was called to the tee at Formby for the first qualifying round he was embarking on the first 18 holes of his life.

On the first two holes his marker lost count of Maurice's earnest endeavours and gave him the benefit of the doubt, marking him for an 11 and a 12. The total came to 121 and Maurice put his finger squarely on the problem: 'At the start I was trying too hard. By the end of the round I felt that I was beginning to put it all together.' The evidence supported his diagnosis since his halves read 61, 60. This time the R&A was spared further embarrassment. Flitcroft withdrew from the competition with dignity: 'I have no chance of qualifying.' A reporter who went to the Flitcroft home that evening said to his mother: 'I have called about Maurice and the Open Championship.'

'Oh yes,' she replied with excitement. 'Has he won?'

TIGER WOODS HAS CHANGED GOLF

by Ian Wooldridge

Little has changed since IW's article to challenge his view of Tiger Woods.

Dateline: Augusta 2002

At high noon at the Augusta National Camp Golf Club yesterday, the consensus was that only one of three factors could conspire against Tiger Woods winning the US Masters.

These were an overnight close family bereavement, a car crash or wrongful arrest by a myopic local cop.

Well, he won, and with it the staggering achievement of four Major championship victories in succession after one of the most thrilling afternoons golf has ever seen.

But win or lose, one result was guaranteed: the biggest audience ever to watch live golf on television in America.

TV executive Dick Ebersol said: 'Even when Tiger plays in an ordinary weekend tournament, the audience shoots up by an extra million. With all the history hanging on these final 18 holes, we're confidently expecting an extra three million.'

'The only sportsman you can now compare him with is Muhammad Ali. Tiger has become the most instantly recognized athlete in the world today.'

His impact on the sport is so immense that he attracts not only already dedicated golf fans, but casual viewers fascinated by the young black man who, in four years, has turned the most conservatively traditional of games on its head.

Blacks are now tuning into telecasts of a sport which, until recently, was predominantly a pastime for the white and wealthy. So are women.

Naturally the television companies, their commercial advertisers and particularly Nike, the sports equipment manufacturers who perceptively signed Woods on an exclusive $100 million contract in 1997, are ecstatic. Ironically, so are Woods' fellow American tournament golfers.

Apart from those in immediate contention for yesterday's Green Jacket and the $1,008,000 purse that went with it, all were hoping, if not actually praying, for a Woods victory.

The tough Hal Sutton, tied in 25th place and a doomed 10 shots off the pace yesterday, was both generous and philosophical.

'I want him to be the best there's ever been because he's driving the game,' he said.

He didn't actually admit that the rest were hanging on Woods' flying coat tails, but that's what he meant.

Little wonder. In 1996, before Woods turned professional, the cumulative prize money from 45 events on the American circuit was $69 million. This year it has almost trebled to $185 million.

Even last year, 45 US players each took home more than £1 million.

Last year, Sutton outfought Woods to win the Players' Championship by one shot, but there were no hard feelings because he was well down the field here in Augusta.

'Most other American sports are spiralling downwards,' said Sutton. 'Golf has taken off and believe me it's down to one man.'

This unprecedented boom, even at a time when the American economy is trembling, has reached every level of the game.

Flying over America now you expect to see nothing more than neatly mown fairways and sand bunkers. It has 17,100 golf courses and 10 new ones are being opened every week.

Alongside arts and science diplomas, eight universities are now offering degrees in golf. More than 1,400 students are already enrolled in courses which embrace playing, agronomy, clubhouse management and, for the dunces, caddying.

Woods is too self-contained and intelligent publicly to attribute any of this phenomenon to himself. He has a nine-man management team to handle his business affairs and two discreet bodyguards permanently in attendance. Tiger, with those hooded eyes, simply plays the golf and, after some indiscretions in the early days, avoids all controversy. Celebrity in America has its perils.

If the pressure of incessant public curiosity and scrutiny does not force him into early retirement, I believe we are witnessing the career of·a man who, at 25, will become the wealthiest sportsman of all time.

After watching sport for more than 40 years, I, too, believe he stands at the shoulder of Muhammad Ali.

15

GAME FOR A LAUGH

'I always keep a supply of stimulants handy in case I see a snake, which I also keep handy.'
W. C. FIELDS, putting whisky in his golf bag.

Some of you about to take up the game of golf may be surprised to know that over the years probably more humour has been extracted from the game and those who play it than any other sport. However, if you do a little detective work, you'll soon discover that cricket, soccer and boxing all have their place, but it won't take you long to discover there is a definite dearth of tennis, hockey and lacrosse jokes! As for badminton or bowls, I don't think I've ever heard one!

Over the years I've been bombarded by people sending poems, stories, many varied, weird and wonderful ideas and I'm taking this occasion to introduce you to one or two that have given me a smile. After all, anything that puts a smile on the face of a Grumpy Old Man has to be a good thing.

Rather like the letters read out by Sir Terry Wogan on his Radio 2 morning programme, many of them start off sounding genuine, but have a punch line that can be dangerous, so you have to do a bit of editing along the way! Here's an example: whilst living in Leeds, at Moor Allerton Golf Club, just on the north side of that fair city, I received this letter in a very impressive envelope, with 'The Rescue Mission, Birmingham' printed boldly on the back. It read:

Dear Mr Alliss,

Perhaps you've heard of me and my nationwide campaign in the cause of Temperance. Each year for the past fourteen, I have made a tour of Scotland and the north of England, including Manchester, Glasgow and your town of Leeds, where I have delivered a series of lectures on the Evils of Drink. On this tour I have been accompanied by a young friend and assistant, David Powell. David, a young man from a good family, with an excellent background, is a pathetic example of a life ruined by excessive indulgence in alcohol and, may I add, women of a loose nature!

David would appear with me at lectures and sit on the platform wheezing, just staring at the audience through bleary, bloodshot eyes, sweating profusely, picking his nose, sometimes passing wind and making obscene gestures, while I would point out that he was an example of what drinking can do to a person.

Unfortunately, last summer David died. A mutual friend has given me your name and I wonder if you would care to take David's place on the next Tour?

Yours, in faith,

Reverend Rupert R. Knight

Rescue Mission

Much has been made of the introduction in 2008 of drug testing for golfers, both men and women. I'm not quite sure how it's going to work. To my full knowledge no pill has been invented that makes you a better putter, one who never misses from four feet or slices a drive away right out of bounds when the wind is blowing from left to right. But years ago, when the first serious campaigns began in an attempt to stop people smoking, many ideas were suggested to stop the craving. A friend of mine from Bournemouth reported that his regular golfing partner had given up smoking and was living on Polo mints and his game was improving! So I was amused to get the following:

R&A Committee (Rules)
Fox House
Glacier Street
Bournemouth

Subject: Investigation into the use of drugs as applied to mid-handicap, upper/lower quartile age group, golfers to identify the organic digestive bowelic inhibitive addictive sexualist effects thereof.

Sir
My Committee has instructed me to write to you re the above – as it applies to yourself.

It has been brought to our attention that you are in the habit – during actual play – of eating/sucking/crunching a proprietary brand of mint commercially sold as 'Polo'.

While this activity may on the surface appear to be quite innocuous, I have to bring to your attention that the fact that as the aforementioned mint may contain up to 0.00183mg/csl (by volumetric ratio) of the substance dihexythedrylanicmexain, it can under certain conditions, viz. before, during, after or instead of alcohol or sex – or in moments of high emotional stress, e.g. first tee on Sunday morning – be considered to be a drug within the meaning of the Act.

Although legally speaking the intake of such artificial aids does not at this moment contravene the R&A Rules, such actions are not considered to be in the best interests of the game.

Having read reports regarding your standard of play, my Committee accepts that you are obviously in need of something to counteract the depressive nature of your normal game. However, whilst we have no statutory powers to order you to stop taking this power-driving, one-putting aid, we would urge you to:

(a) limit your intake to the hours of bunker play;
(b) resist the temptation to whistle through the centre hole whilst your opponent is on his backswing;
(c) at least hand the bloody things round.

I am, Sir, your obedient servant,
Ivor Trebor

It is hardly surprising in such a popular and well promoted game that golf clubs – whether they be of the grandest nature or a modest, family-owned, nine-hole knock-about little course, tucked away in some unfashionable corner of the world – do produce surprising moments. Here are a couple of examples that made me smile.

Two professional friends of mine were attached to clubs at both ends of England. First of all, Hugh Lewis, who, for so many years, was the major domo at the Altrincham Municipal, some seven or eight miles south of Manchester. It was a very busy club and of good quality, well cared for, considering the amount of golf played there. Two occasions come to mind, one when he looked out of the shop window, to see a youngish man pushing a pram up the fairway, parking it gently by the side of the green, taking a putter which lay across the chassis, putting out, then moving on to the next tee. Hugh couldn't resist asking him what was going on and was told that his wife didn't like him to go out to play golf and the only way he could escape her clutches was to say he'd take the baby for a walk, which he did. He hoped it was all right, and he knew that he shouldn't wheel the pram on to the greens. Hugh sent him on his way, with a smile (and a prayer!).

On another occasion he caught a golfer picking up divots, examining them and then placing them in his golf bag. It turned out he'd just moved to the town and had a very small area of ground between his front gate and front door. He was collecting divots to create a small lawn, one about three foot by seven foot and he hoped it was okay to take them for he'd noticed divots didn't grow back very often! Well, what do you say?

Down in Bournemouth there is a very attractive municipal course called Meyrick Park, which for many years was the home of John Stirling, a Glaswegian with a wonderful sense of humour. John was a good player but was also building a reputation as an excellent teacher. Practice facilities at the club were meagre, although he had taken over a neglected room in the basement of the clubhouse, where he strung up a net, put down a couple of mats and could, when the weather was bad, administer aid under cover. His fame grew and he thought it might not be a bad idea to find some other accommodation round town where he could give evening classes. You know the sort of thing, a village hall, school gymnasium, etc. So a small advert was placed in the *Bournemouth Echo* advertising group lessons – and off he went.

He soon realised newcomers to the game had no clubs so he accumulated about thirty seven-irons, some were ladies' length, some in better condition than others, they could have been created by Heinz, for there were at least 57 varieties! He kept them in a huge, rather dilapidated leather golf bag in the back shop. They stood him in good stead through the winter months, but when the clocks went forward the bag was left in the corner, ready to be dusted down for next winter's activities. One day John had played eighteen holes in the morning, gone off for a sandwich and a cup of tea; when he returned he noticed the big bag was missing. Now John had just employed a new young assistant, a keen young lad who was anxious to please. John enquired where the bag of seven-irons had disappeared to.

'Well, boss, we've had a lot of people in today wanting to hire clubs and the big bag was the only one left, so a fellow paid me the money and he's gone off with them.' John's face was a picture. 'You mean he didn't ask you any questions?' 'No, not at all I think it was his first game on a proper golf course.' John waited and waited for the man to return, wondering what on earth his comments would be. At last a youngish man hoved into view, sweating profusely, and brought the clubs back into the shop, to be met by cheerful John, who said, 'How was that, did you enjoy yourself?' 'Yes,' he said, 'I had a great time. The game's a bit more difficult than I thought, it's the first time I've ever been round 18 holes. It took quite some time and I lost a few balls but it was most enjoyable.' 'Were the clubs all right?' asked John. 'Oh yes, they were great! Only one thing though, I could have done with one of those flat ones.' I presume he meant a putter!

On another occasion, and I can't remember the course, but the first hole was a blind drive over the top of a hill, on the crest of which was a ten-foot-high pole stuck in the middle of the fairway indicating the direction. Well, a couple of newcomers stepped on to the first tee, having never been on that or any other course before, played solemnly to the marker post, struggled to lift it out of the ground (rather like those giant cabers tossed at the Highland Games), played out the hole which had grass about six inches high round the aperture. Then, due to the hole being three foot deep, couldn't get the ball out of the hole, so went back to the clubhouse to complain!

Some years ago I received a letter from Mr Roy Richardson of Kempsey, near Worcester. He was a member of the Senior Section of the Puckrup Hall Golf Club near Tewkesbury. He thought the following 'Golfer's Prayer' would amuse me:

The pro is my shepherd, I shall not slice,
He maketh me drive straight down the green fairways,
He leadeth me across the still water hazards,
He restoreth my approach shots,
He leadeth me down the paths of accuracy for my game's sake.
Yea, though I chip through the rough in the shadow of the sand traps,
I fear no bogeys, for his advice is with me.
He prepareth a strategy for me in the presence of my opponents,
He anointeth my head with confidence.
The cup will not run over,
Surely birdies and eagles shall follow me all the rounds of my life
And I will score in the low 80s for ever.

During my life as a club professional, two very happy periods at Parkstone and Moor Allerton, one of my assistants was a young man called Derrick Kulher. He had a waspish sense of humour and a quick wit. One day we were sitting in the clubhouse and heard this piece coming over the radio that was rather creepy and sentimental to say the least. It was just called 'The Deck of Cards.' It had a religious theme, which had been put together in a clever way, but it was a bit OTT. Anyway, Derrick thought he would do his own version and here it is:

In the Italian Campaign a group of soldiers had been on the march for several days. They came across a small town called Cassino. As it was Sunday they all went to church. The service began and they took out their prayer books, all except one man, a coloured Jewish Eskimo, who took out a golf bag and began chipping balls into the font. 'Soldier!' ordered the sergeant, who was also Jewish, 'Put those clubs away immediately.'

After the service the soldier was brought before his CO who said, 'I hope you have an explanation for playing golf in church, and also a letter from your Secretary, otherwise I shall punish you as no man has been punished before.' 'Sir,' said the soldier, 'we've been on the march for six days now and I have no bible or prayer book, only my golf bag. You see, when I take out my driver I think of the Israelites being driven out into the wilderness. When I take out my three-iron, with its heel and toe balancing and bigger "sweet" spot, I remember that God has a big sweet spot for everyone. When I take out my five-iron I think of the Ten Commandments, well, half of them. With my six-iron I remember the parable of the wise virgins, six made the party and six weren't really virgins at all, just a bunch of girls up from Jerusalem on a hot-dogger. When I take out my waterproofs I'm reminded that God will protect me from everything. When I look at my scorecard I think of confession, and when I stand down-wind of my caddy I'm reminded of the stable where Jesus was born. So you see, sir, my golf bag has served me as a bible, a prayer book, as well as a golf bag.'

The soldier was court-martialled for gross insolence and given a choice of sentence. Either he could face a firing squad or be sent for ten years of listening to Harry

Carpenter playing excerpts from Handel's Messiah on a set of engine tappets and a spring compressor.

I know that was true because I was the vicar.

Well, he was only twenty-two at the time!

I like the story the late Ben Sayers Snr, a great player and club-maker from North Berwick, related, how he sold two left-handed and two right-handed clubs to a rather snooty American visitor who seemed to think the game of golf was rather beneath him. Several hours later the American marched up to Sayers and complained bitterly that he'd been made a fool of. 'Oh, no, sir,' said Sayers. 'What you do is, you take the right-handed clubs for holes going out and then you change over and use the left-handed ones coming in.' Exit one puzzled American!

This one is not about humour, it's about personalities. It was in the early 1930s that a certain pilot officer, Douglas Bader, a daring flyer and once brilliant at rugby and cricket, had a terrible crash at the Woodley aerodrome near Reading, the results of which meant the amputation of his right leg above the knee, and his left leg below the knee. At the Roehampton Hospital they fitted him with a pair of metal legs. From there he did quite amazing things, apart from learning to walk; he was able to drive a car, play some golf and even pilot an aeroplane. The RAF would not take him back in peacetime, although they were mighty glad to see him in 1939 when he rejoined and had the most astonishing exploits as a fighter pilot.

It took him quite some time to get acclimatised to the game of golf. The first time he went out to hit a few balls he fell over umpteen times. He tried a slower, less dramatic swish at the ball, and suddenly he began to hit it quite nicely and remain on his feet. Golf became an obsession. He used to practise at the delightful North Hants Golf Club, and it wasn't long before he harnessed some of his old sporting skills. He had a fine co-ordination of eye and a steely determination. Soon he could play three, six, nine holes and then finally up to eighteen. He began to go round in under 100. His first wife, Thelma, was an enthusiastic caddy and his main source of encouragement. His handicap came down to 18 and he was playing in quite a number of competitions.

It was while he was at North Hants he met Henry Longhurst, who at that time was a very good amateur player and had just started his career by becoming the chief golf writer for *The Sunday Times*, where he stayed for more than twenty years. In 1936 Henry had won the German Amateur Championship and had a keen eye for a talented player, and was most impressed when, in his company, Bader went round in 81. They played together a number of times, and it was during these pleasant interludes that Henry made a study of Bader's extraordinary game.

Bader had already persuaded the Roehampton Limb Clinic to 'tune' his legs so that they were more adapted to the game of golf. The clinic fitted a sort of universal joint in each ankle, which gave him the lateral freedom he needed to straddle his legs, placing both feet flat on the ground, whereas previously he had been tilted, rather uncomfortably, against the inside of his shoes. Longhurst noted that Bader struck the ball particularly well when playing shots on fairways that sloped gently uphill. In fact he thought the uphill lie made it easier for Bader to get squarely in behind the ball. He discussed this and agreed it would be an ingenious move to take half an inch off one leg so that Bader could enjoy the same effect on level ground! 'Wish I could do the same,' grunted Longhurst.

Bader took the proposition to Roehampton but they feared shortening one leg could create a bend in his spine. Bader said he'd risk that, his golf mattered so much. So the leg was trimmed, and to good effect. Bader felt better for it and his golf improved.

When Longhurst heard the news he wrote a piece in his paper about the man who had removed half an inch from his left leg so he could play golf from 'a permanent uphill lie'. When he saw the article Bader rang Longhurst in a state of great excitement. 'You old goat,' he said, 'I had it taken it off my right leg, not the left one.' There was silence for a moment then, 'Good God,' said Henry, 'you've taken half an inch off the wrong leg!'

Douglas Bader was a good friend of my father and I had the privilege of spending quite a bit of time in his company. He participated in one of the thirty-six programmes I did entitled *Around with Alliss* and also competed at least once in our *Pro-Celebrity* series from the Turnberry Hotel. It was there, whilst playing the 10th hole, in an attempt to get into a bunker short of the green, he fell over. There he was, lying on his back, like a turtle, arms and legs flailing in the air. I and several others made an attempt to get into the bunker to give him a helping hand, to which his second wife Joan said sharply, 'Leave him, leave him. He won't thank you for it!' And, sure enough, he edged round and eventually got to his feet, rather flushed, and was pulled up out of the bunker.

It was obvious that he wasn't very well, so that particular game ended and he was driven back to the clubhouse, where a doctor was called. This was about 3 p.m. About seven o'clock Douglas came down into the Marley hospitality room (Marley being our very gracious sponsors) to loud applause and in his usual bluff and noisy way said, 'I don't know what all the fuss was about. Can't a fellow slip up now and again without the whole bloody world knowing about it?'

As it turned out, it was probably a mini heart attack; two or three years later he sadly suffered a major one and died. He was a totally remarkable, if irascible, character. They certainly don't make 'em like that nowadays! In any war I'd pay a lot to have him on my side.

16

TRIUMPH OF THE GRUMPY OLD MAN

'The last time I played a round with Vice President Agnew he hit a birdie – an eagle, a Moose, an Elk and a Mason.'
BOB HOPE

And so, as Bernard Darwin might put it, perhaps it is time for tea. We have seen how the phenomenon of the Grumpy Old Man has been recognised, even if it is not restricted to the old or just one gender, and despite initial appearances to the contrary, golf can play a part in exorcising the demons created by modern life. I hope, by reading this book, your interest in golf might have been rekindled or that you might be encouraged to try this wonderful game for the first time. It has certainly given me lifelong pleasure, brought me into contact with the most interesting people, allowed me to witness some of the most memorable moments, and all mixed with a large dose of the weird and wonderful.

Over the years I have had an amazing collection of proposals sent to me: ideas on how the Rules of Golf could be changed to make them simpler to understand and implement; new structures for golf club membership; new dress codes so men could walk into their club sporting off the shoulder shirts in competition with the younger, sexier lady members (and also no socks!); ideas for improving television coverage; plus the odd cake – probably a legacy from cricket commentaries on Test Match Special.

I received one missive recently I thought might amuse, particularly older members, probably at this very moment sitting in a comfortable chair looking out at a dismal scene and thinking how unfair life is. Well, here are a few thoughts to ponder for those of you born before the end of the 1960s (and believe it or not I'm in that bracket):

Firstly we survived being born to mothers who smoked and/or drank, and we lived in houses made of asbestos. We took aspirin, ate blue cheese, raw egg products, loads of bacon and processed meat, tuna from a can, and after the trauma of birth, our baby cots were covered with brightly coloured, lead-based paints. There were no child-proof lids on medicine bottles or locks on doors or cabinets, and when we rode our bicycles we had no helmets; most of the time no shoes; not to mention the risks taken when hitch-hiking. We would ride in cars with no seat belts or airbags (unheard of!), riding in the back of an estate car or pick-up truck on a warm day; or on the wheel arch when one of the green-keepers was cutting the fairways; driving that old Fordham tractor was a delight, with the wind in our hair and the smell of new-mown grass – what a treat. We drank water from the garden hose; takeaway food was limited to fish and chips – there were no pizzas, McDonald's, KFCs and the like. Even though most of the shops closed at six o'clock and didn't open over the weekends, we didn't starve to death. We shared one soft drink with our friends, drinking from the same bottle, and nobody died. It was quite fun to collect old bottles and cash them in at the corner shop to buy Wilson's toffees and some bubblegum; we ate cup-cakes, white bread and real butter; we had soft drinks with sugar in. Not many of us were overweight, I suppose because we were outside playing. Bullies always ruled the playground at school, some got their comeuppance; the idea of our parents bailing us out if we broke the law was unheard of, some of them actually sided with the authorities! Children didn't have strange names like Vanilla, Kiaora, Blade, Bluebell, Tiddlywinks and others too complicated to mention. Remember, this generation produced some of the best risk-takers, problem-solvers and inventors that have ever been.

We are survivors: We got married first, then lived together, how quaint!

A Big Mac was an oversize raincoat.

Crumpet was what we had for tea.

We existed before House Husbands and Computer Dating.

Sheltered accommodation was where you waited for a bus.

We were there before day-care centres, group homes and disposable nappies.

We never head of FM radio, tape-decks, artificial hearts, word processors, or young men wearing earrings – that all went out with Sir Walter Raleigh 400 years ago.

A chip was a piece of wood or fried potato.

Hardware was nuts and bolts,

And software – well, no such word.

Before 1940 'Made in Japan' meant junk.

The term 'making out' referred to how well you did in your exams.

Stud was something that fastened a collar to a shirt, and

Going all the way meant staying on a double-decker bus right into the terminus.

Grass was mown,

Coke was kept in a cool spot.

A joint was a piece of meat you ate, if you were lucky, on Sundays, and

Pot was something you cooked in.

Rock music was a fond mother's lullaby.

A gay person was the life and soul of the party.

Aids just meant beauty treatment or help for someone in trouble.

There were no radar, credit cards, laser beams, ball-point pens, dishwashers, tumble dryers, electric blankets, air conditioners, drip-dry clothes, and

Man had not walked on the moon.

We had freedom, failure, success and responsibility, and we learnt to deal with it all.

And you're one of them. Congratulations! You had the luck to grow up before the lawyers and various governments regulated our lives for our own good!

Our children should realise how brave their parents were! It really is a triumph for the Grumpy Old Man just to keep going, always ready to head to the next tee, you might say. And who would have thought that, all along, golf was the secret cure?

17

GLOSSARY

Address To take up a stance and ground the club before striking.

Albatross Taking three strokes under par for the hole.

Apron The area around the green that is not mown quite as closely as the green itself.

Birdie Taking one stroke under par for the hole.

Bisque Stroke conceded in form of a handicap.

Bogey Now taken to mean, especially in America, one stroke over par. It is still used to mean a par, particularly by older golfers.

Borrow Allowance needed on a putt that is not going to run straight towards the hole, usually because of the gradient of the green.

Bunker A deliberate hazard, either an area of bare ground, or more usually a depression that is filled with sand.

Caddie One who carries or handles a player's clubs and otherwise assists him.

Carry The distance between the point of the hitting of ball and its first bounce on landing.

Casual water Temporary accumulation of water.

Chip A low running approach to the flag made from close to the green.

Cut-up High shot played with side spin.

Divot Small strip of turf taken out of the ground in playing iron shots.

Dogleg Shape of a hole turning from left to right or right to left.

Dormie Term used in matchplay when a player is as many holes up as there holes left to play.

Draw A shot, made intentionally, which, for a right-hander, bends slightly to the left.

Eagle Taking two strokes under par for the hole.

Fade A shot which, when hit by a right-hander, is intentionally bent slightly to the right.

Fairway The specially prepared area of turf between tee and green.

Forward press A slight movement forward of the hands before beginning the back swing when putting.

Fourball A match in which four players compete, each playing with his own ball.

Foursome A match in which four players compete in pairs, each playing alternate shots with the same ball. Sometimes used to describe four players playing together.

Green The part of a golf hole specially prepared for putting.

Greensome A variation of foursomes in which each player is allowed to hit from the tee, the best shot then being selected.

Handicap System of awarding bonus strokes which enable golfers of differing levels to meet on equal terms.

Hole The playing area from tee to green.

Honour A player entitled to play first from the tee through having won the previous hole is said to have the honour.

Hook A shot which when hit by a right-hander curves to the left; more pronounced than a draw and unintentional.

Iron The club, the head or striking part of which is made of metal.

Matchplay The method of deciding a match by the number of holes won, as distinct from the number of strokes taken in a round.

Medal play (also **strokeplay**) A match or competition decided by the number of strokes taken in a round and not by the number of holes won.

Par The number of strokes required by a first-class player at each hole.

Pitch A lofted approach shot to the green.

Pitch and run A shot pitched and allowed to run up to the flag.

Pull A straight-flying shot which, when hit by a right-hander, goes to the left of the line intended.

Push A straight-flying shot which, when hit by a right-hander, goes to the right of the line intended.

Rough The area within the course not specially prepared for play and cut only occasionally.

Run of the green When a ball in motion is stopped or deflected by an outside agency.

Sand wedge A broad-soled club mainly used for playing from sand.

Scratch A handicap of nought.

Semi-rough Rough bordering the fairway cut to a height of approximate two to four inches.

Slice A shot which, when hit by a right-hander, curves to the right; more pronounced than a fade and unintentional.

Stance To take up position before hitting a shot.

Strokeplay (see **medal play**).

Wedge A broad-soled iron having maximum loft for hitting short high shots, usually to the green.

Woods Clubs with large heads to achieve distance; once made of solid wood, but now with hollow metal heads.